iWITNESS

INTERDISCIPLINARY INVESTIGATIONS

THE MIDDLE AGES

CREATING AN ENVIRONMENT

Dale Crooke

Steve Frick

Moya Hanaway

Carolyn Major-Harper

Sarasota Middle School
Sarasota, Florida

D. C. Heath and Company

TEACHER'S TEAM PLANNING GUIDE

FOREWORD

THIS RESOURCE UNIT

allows you to teach the content you know, while collaborating with your colleagues.

Making an interdisciplinary approach work within the realities of your school day is our main goal; therefore, we've striven to make the possibilities and roles for each discipline apparent. But many other possibilities and combinations of roles are possible. By using the Team Planning Guide, you'll undoubtedly come up with new connections and new combinations of roles to suit your own needs and expertise.

gives you the process and the tools to create an interdisciplinary unit your students won't soon forget!

The Planning Guide is designed to provide you with a step-by-step process for thinking through and putting together a unit that meets YOUR needs—year after year.

acknowledges the resources you already have in your classroom.

We've taken into account what is typically taught in middle school science, math, English, literature, and social studies. You'll be able to take advantage of the resources you already have in your classroom.

has been created and used by an interdisciplinary team of teachers.

An interdisciplinary team from Sarasota, Florida developed a unit on the Middle Ages for their own students; the team then worked with D.C. Heath to brainstorm, expand, and write this unit. Throughout this Planning Guide, you'll see the thoughts, ideas, and advice of the team, as well as comments from individual team members.

Photo Credits

16: German Information Service
20: The Pierpont Morgan Library, New York. M.399, f.5v.
39: Photofest

Published simultaneously in Canada

Printed in the United States of America

International Standard Book Number: 0-669-32217-2

1 2 3 4 5 6 7 8 9 10 BAW 99 98 97 96 95 94

CONTENTS

GETTING ACQUAINTED

A recipe for success!

Hear Ye! Hear Ye!

Fair Damsels and brave Knights, gather ye round and meet the Spinnaker Team.

The Spinnakers hail from Sarasota, Florida, where we have been a teaching team since August of 1982. The members of our team are Dale Crooke, Steve Frick, Moya Hanaway, and Carolyn Major-Harper. We love teaching together!

DALE CROOKE was the impetus behind Sarasota's first Medieval unit, and the heroine of the modern fairy tale at the right. This unit grew out of her conviction that kids need to experience history, not just read about it. Over the past eight years, the team has proven that her strategy is both workable and highly effective. Each spring the team's students recreate a little of the Middle Ages in Sarasota, Florida, based on sound instruction, but brought to life with the kind of energy only kids can bring to a project. To students at Sarasota, the Medieval life isn't some alien, distant thing—it's something they've experienced "first-hand"!

STEVE FRICK teaches math, a subject some people would not associate with the Middle Ages. He's happy to prove them wrong: the Middle Ages saw the adoption of Arabic numerals by Europeans, setting the stage for the discoveries of the Renaissance and the Enlightenment. Can you imagine Newton making his calculations with Roman numerals? Neither can Steve. Besides his math skills, Steve brings to the team a special expertise in technology and a taste for precision. The team calls him "Mr. Perfectionist." He's also the reigning Human Checkers Champion.

MAYA HANAWAY is sometimes considered the "Pollyana" of the group, but she does have one strict rule: no dangling participles! She's the language arts teacher and the team's chief motivator, urging both her colleagues and her students on. But she's a doer, too. Her remarkable banner paintings won this accolade from one student: "Who painted the carpet?" She also has an outrageous sense of humor that helps keep everyone working happily. Her suggestions for both instructional and student activities will show you how rich a language arts subject the Middle Ages can be.

CAROLYN MAJOR-HARPER is the team's science teacher, but she's a technology neophyte. She leaves that to Steve—a good example of how team teaching allows teachers to complement one another. Her "stress-free" attitude is one of the group's biggest assets, and a definite help in her role as field trip coordinator. (Not that traveling with a group of middle school students could be stressful.) Like Dale, she believes the key to learning is experience—in science as well as in the humanities. In the pages that follow, you'll find everything the team has discovered about experience-based learning.

A MODERN FAIRY TALE

Once upon a time (1986), in a faraway kingdom, there lived a wild, crazy, creative social studies teacher who pestered her beloved family (teaching team) to have a "real" Medieval Fair. The family merely scoffed and laughed and secretly made faces at her behind her back.

Unbeknownst to the family, she quietly plotted and set out to do it anyway. The children of the kingdom fell under her Merlinesque spell and began to transform ordinary objects (cardboard refrigerator cartons) into castles and shoppes for food, beverages, entertainment, and crafts.

The spell began to seep into other parts of the kingdom when the newly designed refrigerator boxes began appearing in other sections of the family's domain. The children of the kingdom were so enthusiastic about their fair that they conspired to cast the spell on the grown-ups. Then the grown-ups cast the spell even farther by inviting other kingdoms (school teams) to come spend a day at the fair.
From that day to this, the fair has been an Annual Magical Event.

THE END

The Moral Is...

Although we've called it a fairy tale, the story you've just read is true. Our unit—The Middle Ages: Creating an Environment—evolved from this first Medieval Fair experience. We've created some other interdisciplinary units, but this one remains a favorite among both teachers and students. When kids are involved in such an experience, they are learning more than they ever could from a text. They become happy, eager students. In Sarasota, we use the unit with sixth-graders. But we are convinced that it would work just as well with students at other grade levels.

AND THE PLAYERS ARE...

In a typical year, there are 125 students on our team. They are grouped heterogeneously and thus have a wide range of abilities and interests. But there's such a variety of activities in our unit—and such a range of possibilities—that everyone becomes actively involved.

The Middle Ages was once viewed as a time of cessation of learning and growth. (It was even called "The Dark Ages.") However, historians now look at the Midde Ages as a period of great beginnings that links ancient times and our modern world. As students explore these great beginnings, they will discover exciting new facts about events in the Middle Ages and what life was like "back then." They will role play a person who lived during Medieval times. In so doing, they will recreate an interdependent society and demonstrate the self-sufficient attitudes that led to so many inventions and customs.

Since social studies provides the impetus for our unit, that subject area lends itself to the use of an academic student contract. Students must be able to work in cooperative groups and use decision-making skills to plan and carry out a culminating activity (such as a fair, a banquet, a game, or a scrapbook).

SETTING THE SCENE

This unit—as with any interdisciplinary unit—assumes that certain skills already have been taught to students. We recommend that students receive instruction in the following areas, either prior to or during the course of the Middle Ages unit. This will help students experience the joys of success as they recreate their Medieval environments.

LANGUAGE ARTS

Speaking Skills: Students need to feel comfortable and have experience presenting material in front of groups.

Writing Skills: Students need to be able to express themselves in writing, using standard English guidelines.

Comparing/Contrasting: Students need to be able to demonstrate relationships, using similarities and differences.

Evaluating: Students need to know how to use guidelines generated by themselves and by their teachers to assess performance.

MATHEMATICS

Ratio and Proportion: Students need to be familiar with these concepts in order to apply them to scale drawings and/or three-dimensional models.

Measurement: Students should be able to use measuring tools for application on drawings, models, and possible site measurement.

Fractions: Students should have a basic knowledge of fractions when taking measurements and making scale drawings.

Graphing: Students should be able to represent data on various kinds of graphs, including line, picture, bar, and circle.

SCIENCE

Process Skills: Students need to know the process skills and how they are used in a science lesson.

Scientific Method: Students should be familiar with the steps of the scientific method and be able to implement them.

Demonstrating: Students should be able to differentiate between demonstrating and experimenting. Students must be able to demonstrate orally before a large group.

Experimenting: Students should know how to follow the directions of an experiment and be familiar with the safety rules involved.

Researching: Students should have the ability to find necessary resources and apply them to a given topic.

AS A FINAL WORD...

DON'T PANIC! You already have access to curriculum resource materials that will enable you to teach these skills--if you haven't already done so.

OUR OWN TEAM HISTORY

In 1982, the Sarasota County School Board and community made a commitment to Middle Schools, encompassing grades six through eight. In order to make this huge transition a success, teachers were given a choice of transferring into this new experience or out of it. On our school site, teachers were even allowed to choose the members of their own team. History speaks for itself. After eleven years, we are still together.

Our team name, Spinnaker, was chosen to represent the outstanding, colorful sail often used on sailboats. We were envisioning our first group of sixth-grade students to be outstanding, bright, and colorful; and history has borne this out!

As teachers, we count among our strengths the following: our flexibility and willingness to teach in and out of our assigned teaching roles; our willingness to create new learning experiences for our students and for ourselves; our energetic, unique individualism; our creativity; and our raucous sense of humor. These strengths motivate our students to learn in meaningful ways.

Our team name is also an acronym for students who are:

Special

Proud

Interested

Nice

Neat

Ambitious

Kind

Energetic

Responsible

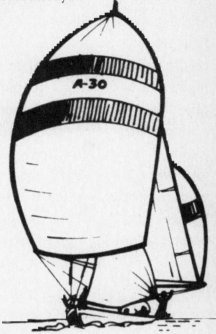

TEAM TIPS

TEAMING—INTERDISCIPLINARY, POSITIVE SUGGESTIONS

✓ Keep a sense of humor.

✓ Create an environment where it is okay to say what you think and show how you feel.

✓ Don't be afraid to say "OOPS."

✓ Take time to step back and take a second look.

✓ Find enjoyment in what you do, and pass that enjoyment on to your students.

SURVEY THE PRODUCTS

The Teacher Team Planning Guide and the Student Project Book work hand-in-hand to help students explore the Middle Ages and to create their own Medieval environments. In their roles as Medieval people, students investigate how their society is organized, how they earn a living, what values and ideas are important to them, and how they will affect the future (our present-day world). Students then use what they have learned to create a Medieval story—which they may present dramatically, in writing, or through graphics.

As you present the instructional activities to students, they are completing the pages of the Student Project Book. Together—the activities and the student project—prepare students for a culminating experience that puts what they have learned into a greater perspective.

TEAM PLANNING GUIDE

A TRIED AND TRUE PLANNING PROCESS
The Planning Guide is organized to reflect the ways teams actually plan and carry out units. You begin by Brainstorming your needs and goals, proceed through Customizing the Unit to suit those specific needs, and wrap up by Evaluating Your Unit.

ACTIVITIES GALORE!
The Activity Bank presents dozens of fully developed activities (Launch, Student Project, Instructional, and Culminating), each of which suggests when you can use it, what you might assess, what Guiding Questions and objectives you can cover, and how to go about doing the activity in your science, social studies, math, English, or literature class.

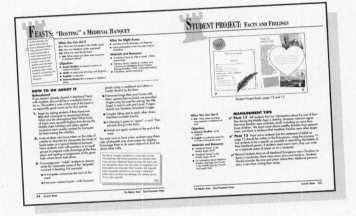

MEETINGS THAT WORK FOR YOU!
Each step of the planning process is supported by a Team Meeting feature. Team meetings provide a way to think about and record all the decisions that an interdisciplinary unit requires. The forms that accompany each team meeting are reproducible so you can make multiple copies of them.

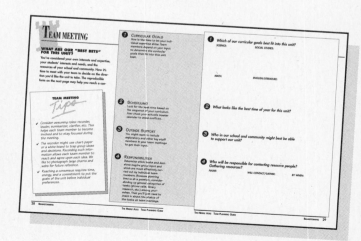

STUDENT PROJECT BOOK

STUDENT PROJECT

The Student Project is designed to help students experience vicariously what life was like during the Middle Ages. In their Medieval roles, students explore many different facets of life during the Middle Ages. They then use the information they have acquired to write a story set in the Middle Ages—with themselves as characters!

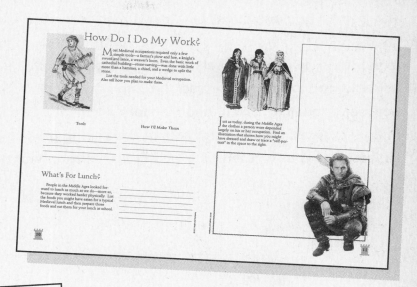

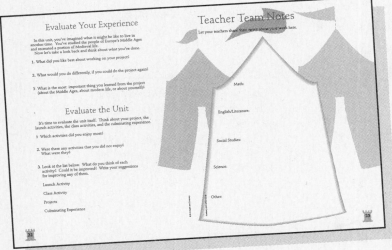

SELF-EVALUATION

After completing their projects, students have an opportunity to evaluate not only their own work and input but evaluate the unit as a whole. Their evaluation is crucial to the way you choose to teach the unit in the future.

THE HERALD

This section of the Student Project Book includes a wealth of information about the Middle Ages. Graphic aids such as maps and time lines help students establish the parameters of their projects. There is a databank of Medieval roles and names and heroes. Excerpts from Medieval literature—together with an extensive bibliography of books— help set the tone of students' stories.

REVIEW THE UNIT

The graphic on these pages provides a quick overview of the unit, showing the flow from launch, through development, to the culminating experience. Two parallel sets of questions guide both the instructional activities and the student project, helping students make the connection between academic content and the more personal viewpoint they explore in their projects. We have found that developing guiding questions such as these keeps us focused on the concepts the team wants to investigate.

LAUNCH

A high-interest, high-energy activity that kicks off your unit and gets kids "hooked."

INSTRUCTIONAL ACTIVITIES	QUESTION	STUDENT PROJECT

Who were the people of the Middle Ages?
In selecting their roles, students investigate who the people of the Middle Ages were. The Herald provides information about nobles and clergy, as well as about peasants, townspeople, and wanderers. It also describes the relationships among these various groups of peoples.

Who are you and where do you live?
Each student takes on the persona of someone who lived during the Middle Ages. The student then chooses a time and place in Medieval Europe as a setting for his or her "story."

How was Medieval society organized?
In addition to information provided in The Herald, several instructional activities are designed to help students understand the organization of Medieval society. For example, students do research about guilds and write journal entries about progress through the stages of apprenticeship, journeyman, and master. They also research the layout and function of Medieval towns.

What are your feudal duties?
As students choose their Medieval roles, they consider how hard people had to work just to meet their basic needs. As they work through the project, they discover how people depended upon each other for their very survival.

INSTRUCTION-AL ACTIVITIES

What was daily life like then?
Numerous instructional activities focus on every-day life in the Middle Ages. Students explore dietary habits and the importance of herbs in preparing foods and in the practice of medicine. Students do research about Medieval trade fairs, as well as about some not-so-ordinary events, such as Viking invasions and the Black Death.

What values and ideas were important in Medieval culture?
Students discover that in the Middle Ages the code of behavior was grounded in religious thought as well as in the Code of Chivalry. They read literature of and about the time as a way to explore the ideas that people felt were important.

How did people in the Middle Ages help shape our world today?
Numerous activities enable students to infer how ideas, values, customs, and practices of Medieval people have influenced our modern world. Students discover that the "middle class" had its beginnings in Medieval society. So did trade unions, crop rotation, the business of banking, Arabic numbers, and the English language.

QUESTION

STUDENT PROJECT

How do you earn a living?
In their Medieval roles, students next select their occupations. They consider the tools they will need to carry out their work. They also describe how they will make those tools. They draw self-portraits to show how they look and dress.

What do you believe in? What is important to you?
After identifying their family ties, students describe their view of the world—what they value, hope for, fear. Students also describe the dwellings in which they live and tell what a typical day in their lives might be like.

What changes, if any, have you seen in your community during your lifetime?
In their Medieval roles, students describe for their children changes thay have witnessed in their lives. They also give eyewitness accounts of extraordinary events they may have experienced. Finally, students write stories about their lives, incorporating what they have learned about life in the Middle Ages.

CULMINATING EXPERIENCE

This experience sums up the entire unit. It is the time for students to apply the content knowledge they've acquired through the instructional activities and the new perspectives they've gained through their projects. It's learning made fun!

PREVIEW THE PROCESS

Now that you have an idea of how the unit works, take a look at the planning process we used to put it together.

■ First we **brainstorm**, often listing on the board each and every idea we have for the unit. After reviewing our ideas (both good and bad), we are better able to decide what our guiding questions will be and what students will do for a project. You'll want to look over our questions and projects to see if you want or need to make any modifications.

■ Next we **customize** the unit for the students we have that year. We first choose the culminating experience–it's what usually excites us and the kids most! Then we select the instructional activities that support our culminating experience and the student project. With these aspects in place, we choose our launch activity.

■ Although **evaluation** comes last in the process, we evaluate our progress as we move through the unit.

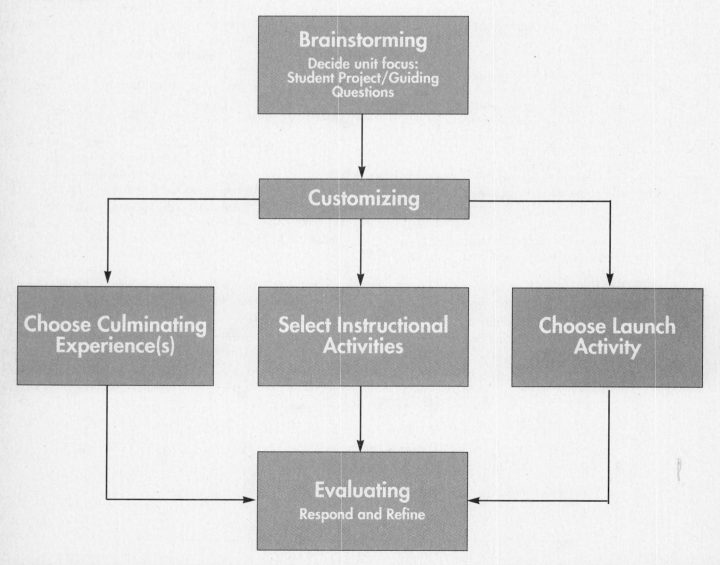

For those of you who like visuals, we've included another flow chart to help you compare the process to the way the unit actually progresses with your students.

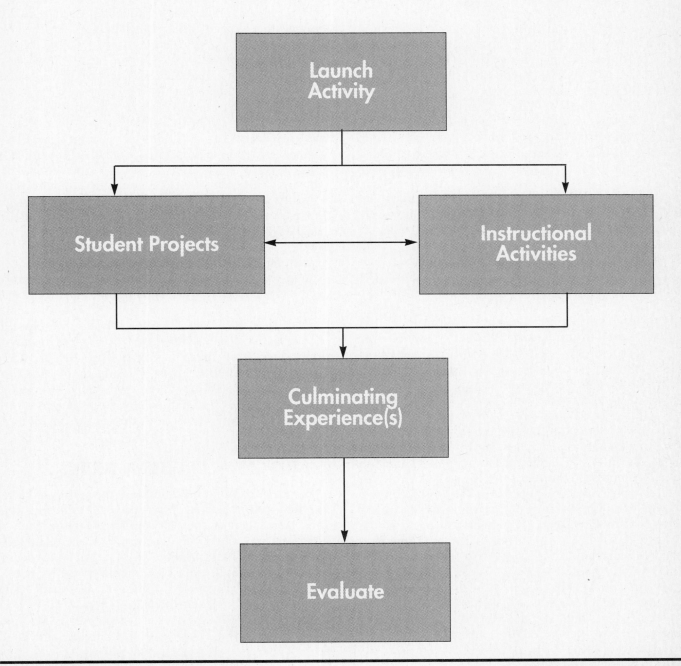

The Middle Ages
AN OVERVIEW

AN END AND A BEGINNING

The origins of the Medieval period lie deep within the era that preceded it. By the year 117 AD Rome's Empire stretched from Spain, Britain, and Gaul to Asia Minor and Palestine. Roman legions had also crossed the Mediterranean and subdued Egypt and much of North Africa.

These conquests posed huge problems. Governing such vast areas was inherently difficult when the fastest means of overland communication was by horse. Since the Empire was built by aggression, there was a constant threat of rebellion in the occupied nations. Things were not well at home, either. Roman landowners imported slaves from the conquered lands, and this caused widespread unemployment. A widening gap between rich and poor was destroying traditional social ties. All these problems contributed to the Empire's decline.

As time went on, Rome's laws were harder to uphold in the distant provinces. Roman society grew more corrupt, and the army began to lose its legendary discipline. Finally even the superb Roman roads throughout Europe fell into disrepair, and as trade stagnated, gold and silver grew scarce. In this weakened condition, the Empire was now vulnerable to attack from the outside.

When these attacks began, they came from several directions. Germanic tribes stepped up their raids against Roman outposts and gradually gained—or regained—control of the left bank of the Rhine River. The Visigoths of Central Europe briefly occupied Rome itself in 410 before invading Gaul and Spain. "Words fail me..." wrote Saint Jerome. "The city which took captive the whole world has itself been captured." The Angles and Saxons pushed the Romans out of the British Isles, and the Vandals set up a new kingdom opposed to Rome in Carthage. From the east came the Huns, who crossed the Alps in 452 and pillaged their way down the Italian peninsula. The most feared invaders were the Vikings of Scandinavia. They used terror as a strategic tactic, leveling one town and taking people captive as a way of extorting ransom from neighboring communities.

This gradual collapse of the Roman Empire set the stage for the Middle Ages. Loosely defined, the Medieval period runs from 500 to 1500 AD. There are, however, events that date the Middle Ages more precisely. Many historians feel the era began in AD 476, when the last Roman Emperor was deposed by the Goth invader Odoacer. Finding an end date is more controversial. Some scholars date the closing of the Middle Ages at 1453, when the Turk Mohammed II conquered Constantinople—the eastern capital of the Roman Empire—and renamed it Istanbul. It makes more sense to say that the Middle Ages ended at different times in different places throughout Europe, as the new period we call the Renaissance gradually took shape.

The Middle Ages are often associated with the cessation of growth and learning. They have been viewed as a "dark age" between the civilization of ancient Rome and modern times. Certainly the chaos of early Medieval Europe contrasts strongly with the achievements of other cultures during the same time. The Medieval Time Line on pages 28 and 29 of the Student Project Book shows that both the Chinese and the Mayans of Central America were enjoying periods of stability and creativity while Europeans were struggling to restore to order. To many Europeans of the early Middle Ages, it must have seemed as though the world was ending. In fact, one world had ended.

But the challenges of the time were met by human courage and resourcefulness. Medieval people struggled to create a new world among the ruins of the old one. They improvised and borrowed from other cultures to meet their immediate needs, and in the process they made important advances. Many of these occurred when ideas from India, China, and the Middle East found their way to Europe, spurring innovations in numerous aspects of life. Those innovations—in everything from farming to philosophy, from navigation to architecture—forged a crucial link in the creation of our world today.

THE TUG OF WAR OF MEDIEVAL POLITICS

As the Pax Romana crumbled, many local rulers attacked their neighbors, hoping to seize their property. In an atmosphere of constant conflict, a network of loyalties and protection was desperately needed, and this gave birth to feudalism. Feudalism began as a system of loyalty among Europe's Germanic tribes. Warriors pledged themselves to a chieftain; in return they received a portion of any goods won in war.

During the 700s, this system changed. As Muslim armies advanced on Europe, leaders offered parcels of

land to those who helped defend their territories. This new system, combining the old Germanic ideals of loyalty to a leader with the exchange of land for protection, came to be called feudalism.

The core of feudalism was an agreement between a landowner, or lord, and a person who promised to help protect his land. This protector was called a vassal. Both lord and vassal were called nobles, a term which originally meant "well-known." When war threatened, local lords entered into alliances with other lords, eventually creating vast networks of interlocking loyalties. Within each network, the leader with the most land and the largest army emerged as king.

At first this arrangement placed most political power in the hands of the local nobility. There were few kings who could exert firm control over a large area (with an occasional exception, such as Charlemagne). But in the twelfth century, the balance began to shift. Strong kings wrestled power away from the nobles of England, France, and Spain. This brought about the creation of the nation-state, a country with a single ruler and a central government.

The formation of nation-states produced mixed reactions among the king's subjects. Many people took pride in sharing a language and culture. Merchants supported these centralized governments because peace and order made it easier to trade. The nobles, naturally, were less enthusiastic. Sometimes they resisted their loss of power.

In England, a group of powerful noblemen forced King John to sign the Magna Carta in 1215. This charter affirmed that the king, too, was governed by the rules of the land. One clause, for instance, stated that the king could not impose taxes without consent from a "counsel of the realm." Although the nobles had conceived the Magna Carta as a check on royal power for their own sake, it formed the basis for laws that protected everyone.

THE PILLARS OF THE MEDIEVAL WORLD: THE SERFS AND PEASANTS

With Europe divided into the patchwork domains of warring nobles, travel and trade became extremely dangerous during the early Middle Ages. Whole communities retreated into self-sufficient units called manors. Part of a manor's land was reserved for the use of the lord; the rest was divided among his subjects. Farming was the manor's main activity, but the people living there also produced almost everything else they needed. Raw materials came from the fields, pastures, or surrounding woods, and emerged from the mill or blacksmith shop or bakery as useful items. Anything unavailable locally—with the exception of salt, an important material for the preservation of food—was usually done without.

Those who worked the manors—the vast majority of the Medieval population—were divided into two groups, the serfs and the peasants. The serf owned no land and was "bound to the soil" of the manor. The peasant, or freeman, owned a small piece of land but paid rent to the lord with goods and services. Peasants often possessed a craft or skill other than farming: they were potters, smiths, millers, weavers, carpenters, bailiffs, or shepherds.

A serf's life was particularly taxing. A male serf could gain his freedom only by marrying a free woman, entering the church, or fleeing his manor for a year and a day. He had to perform the lord's farming, mending, and other tasks before he could attend to his personal needs.

The house of a serf usually had three rooms: a "living" room, a bedroom, and a stable. A vegetable and herb garden grew outside, often along with a few fruit trees and a patch of grass for the cow. Some serfs raised hens, sheep, and even bees for honey. At the end of the day a serf and his family ate a meal of stew, bread and ale. Ironically this was a healthier diet than the nobility's, because it included more vegetables and less meat.

Relentless labor was just one oppressive element in the serf's life. He or she lived according to the lord's wishes, and these could be unjust, dangerous, or fatal. Any crime, for example, carried fantastically harsh penalties. It was common for an accused person to be brought before the lord and have a hot iron placed in his or her hand. If the resulting burn healed in three days, the accused was declared innocent—a primitive lie-detector test few suspects could have passed.

Despite these conditions, serfs found occasions for laughter and enjoyment. Sundays were always free, allowing serfs to attend fairs, weddings, and feast days. Dancing was popular, and some Medieval dances survive to this day. Another source of entertainment was sports. Grown men practiced archery, while boys played a type of football. Other sports included casting heavy stones and wrestling.

The self-sufficient character of the manor generally restricted the horizons of both serfs and peasants. But this did not prevent important improvements in farming. Foremost among these was the heavy plow, pulled either by oxen or by horses. This innovation from eastern Europe slowly spread to the west during the early Middle Ages. Its use was spurred by the introduction of the horse collar, an invention from Asia. Medieval farmers also made discoveries of their own: they developed a system of crop rotation that made their lands far more productive.

The range of knowledge bequeathed to us by Medieval peasantry embraces such diverse things as herbal cures, metal tools, stirrups, cranks, and water power. These were, after all, the people who wove the fabric of Medieval culture.

THE NOBLES: A CLASS OF LANDOWNERS

Although the serfs and peasants worked the land, they owned very little of it. Most land was held by the nobles, the ruling class of lords and vassals. But nobles did far more than simply collect rent from their properties. Because land was under constant threat of attack—first from wandering tribes, then from Muslim armies, later from neighboring lords—landowners spent much of their lives as warriors. Even in peacetime, nobles worked hard to cement alliances and prepare for war.

A noble's life was in some ways an opulent one, but it lacked basic comforts that we take for granted. The noble transacted affairs, held court, and entertained in the castle hall or the manor house. The castle was freezing cold in the winter because it was heated by a single fire in the castle hall. Tapestries were hung on the walls for extra warmth, and the floor might be covered with straw, but the castle never really warmed up until spring came.

Castles were dark places, too, and that must have made the chill seem even worse. Windows were small and high and covered with parchment, cloth, or paper. Candles provided some light, but they were made from animal fats, which gave off a foul smell. Most castles and manor houses contained little in the way of furniture. Only the lord or lady slept in a bed, and only the noble host was lucky enough to possess a chair. (That's

why we still call the person in charge of a meeting or organization the "chairperson.")

Even the diet of the nobility had its pitfalls. Dinner, the most elaborate meal of the day, was "trumpeted" at 10 AM. The table where the lord sat was traditionally placed perpendicular to the others, and a great silver salt cellar was placed there so the nobility could look down on the less exalted diners who sat "below the salt." Good manners required diners to avoid poking their fingers in the food, wiping their knives on the tablecloth, or spitting across the table. Yet the menu—which consisted of meat, white bread, and wine—caused skin troubles, digestive disorders, infections, scurvy, and tooth decay.

Noblemen spent much of their time outdoors, hunting and fighting. In peacetime, the lords participated in mock battles called jousts or tournaments. Noblewomen, who were barred from such activities, practiced the domestic arts. They directed the servants, tended to the children, sewed, and sometimes made medicinal concoctions from herbs.

What do we know about noble children? Like twentieth-century kids, they played with toys or pets, or engaged in games of hide-and-seek. Both boys and girls learned household tasks, such as bed making and waiting on tables, to give them some sense of polite behavior. Later boys might be sent to neighboring castles as pages, to learn social duties and games and begin their military training. Girls, too, were often sent elsewhere for "finishing"—that is, to learn more about domestic tasks. They might also be taught to draw, to play a musical instrument, or to speak other languages.

KNIGHTS AND SQUIRES

The first knights were not nobles, but peasants enlisted by nobles to fight under their banners. The noble supplied the knight's horse and costly armor. When some of these mounted soldiers came to England in the 1060s as part of the Norman invasion, the English called them *cnihts*, an Old English word that means "servant." As time went on, the profession became more desirable, and nobles became knights themselves.

Knighthood by then involved a long process of preparation. Starting at around age seven, the prospective knight served as a page, learning to ride a horse and receiving religious training. He also learned manners, hunting, dancing and, perhaps, reading and writing. By the age of thirteen, the page became a squire. In this capacity, he assisted a knight, looking after his armor and weapons while also learning to use them. He aided the knight at tournaments and followed him into battle.

Finally came the long-awaited day. On the eve of his investiture, the squire bathed, dressed in white, and prayed until dawn. In the morning he was blessed, given a suit of armor, and granted knighthood in a ceremony called an accolade. After being touched on the shoulder by the blade of a sword, he officially became a knight and swore to uphold a code of chivalry:

To be brave,
To maintain the right,
To redress the wrong,
To protect women,
To help those in trouble, and
To show mercy to the weak and defenseless.

A knight who broke this vow was relieved of his knighthood in another ceremony.

When wars became less frequent in the later Middle Ages, knights spent more time at home, and jousting for entertainment took the place of warfare. The lord sent invitations to other lords and set up a tent for his guests to watch the joust. New rules governed the sport, but the codes of honor and chivalry prevailed.

Knights were the most romanticized figures of the Middle Ages. In a more skeptical era, it is easy to belittle their code of conduct or to suspect their motives. Yet there are many accounts of knights who upheld their demanding code in the most extreme circumstances. When King Richard of England was felled by an assassin's arrow in 1199, he had his attacker brought to his deathbed and asked why the man had shot him. The man explained that Richard had once killed his father and brother in battle. Richard forgave his killer and ordered that no revenge be taken against him.

TRADE BUILT THE TOWNS

From about the twelfth century, Medieval life began to change. Trade and travel increased, and communities became less isolated. Why? A big factor was the holy wars, or Crusades, which were initiated by Pope Urban II in 1096. The original goal of these wars was to recapture Jerusalem from the Muslim Turks. Shipload after shipload of Crusaders crossed the Mediterranean or marched overland to the Middle East.

The Crusaders never succeeded in expelling the Turks from Palestine. They did, however, bring back spices, fabrics, and other goods from the Middle East, which stimulated interest in trade with the East. A second stimulus came in the early 1300s, when the Venetian merchant Marco Polo published an account of his travels in China.

As merchants traveled greater distances, they looked for safe locations along their routes where they could make longer stops. To avoid being robbed by bandits, a merchant would usually choose a spot near a castle. These places favored by the merchants began to attract permanent residents, both craftspeople and peasants, and grew into towns. Often such a town ended up with its own charter from the king; this allowed some measure of self-government, including the power to pass laws and tax trade.

A related development was the growth of guilds. These organizations of merchants and craftspeople protected their members, insured quality, and fixed "fair prices." Guild members went through a graduated training process, leading from apprentice to journeyman to master craftsman. Much like unions today, guilds also provided their members with social activities and retirement benefits. Guilds covered a wide spectrum of work, from weaving to cathedral-building.

As the volume of trade grew, credit companies—the ancestors of our modern banks—were formed in some towns. They were owned by merchants who understood the complicated conversion of foreign currency. Coins from every nation in Europe were balanced against standardized weights to determine their value.

The net effect of these changes—the rise of towns, the growth of guilds, and the development of banking—made merchants powerful people. Before long they were investing their profits in land, buildings, and shipping. Much later this rising middle class would undermine the foundations of feudalism itself. For now, though, it gave new vitality to the world of Medieval Europe.

THE UNIFYING FORCE OF THE MIDDLE AGES: THE CHURCH

No account of the Middle Ages can omit the Church. This enormously powerful institution could crown kings and declare war. It also provided social services, including hospitals from which no needy person could be turned away. Equally important, the Church was the only place where a person could get an education or pursue scholarship. By hand-copying books of every kind, the Church's monks preserved the heritage of Greek and Roman civilization.

In addition, monks led the way in developing new technology, especially water power. By the eleventh century, power from water wheels, many of them in monasteries, was grinding grain, pressing wine and olive oil, making cloth, and, even working forges with mechanical bellows.

The Church also made a contribution in philosophy with profound implications for Christian Europe: Thomas Aquinas argued that the age-long conflict between Christian faith and ancient philosophy, with its reliance on reason, was a false one. Instead, he believed, faith and reason should work hand-in-hand. This radical change in Christian thinking helped to liberate the creative forces of the Renaissance and the Industrial Revolution.

The Church had a hierarchy much like feudalism, with local priests reporting to bishops who in turn were supervised by archbishops and cardinals, all under the authority of the Pope in Rome. Because the its law governed marriage, divorce, and wills, the Church

exercised a good deal of power. But that power varied throughout the period. During the early Middle Ages, the Church's authority was undermined by nobles who demanded the right to choose local bishops. Only in 1122 did the nobility agree that the Pope alone could appoint them.

By this time, a process of general reform reinvigorated the Church. Two new monastic orders appeared, the Dominicans and the Franciscans. Unlike previous orders, their members did not retreat from the world—they went out into it, preaching and helping the poor.

Religious belief was the glue that held the culture of the Middle Ages together. Except in Spain, with its large Jewish and Muslim population, nearly all Europe's people were Christians. Non-Christians were either barred from important positions or openly persecuted. In fact, most people had little idea that other religions, or, for that matter, other historical periods, even existed. One illuminated manuscript from about 1250 portraying the battles of the Old Testament shows the ancient Israelites battling on horseback, fully equipped with Medieval armor.

Because religious beliefs were so central to Medieval life, most art was religious, and some of the best art was the churches themselves. In the one hundred years between 1170 and 1270, nearly 500 Gothic churches and cathedrals were built throughout Europe. With thin, carefully buttressed walls, towering arches, and expanses of stained glass, Gothic buildings offered a powerful image of religious faith. The cathedrals also united the various classes of Medieval life, since nobles and merchants, knights and serfs all contributed money and

labor to their construction.

The Church provided opportunities for people who were denied them elsewhere. Abbot Suger of France was a prime example. Born a peasant, he was sent to a monastery school by a local priest. There Suger met a boy his age who happened to be the country's prince. Suger became a monk and later an abbot, the leader of a monastery. He supervised the building of the first Gothic church at St. Denis, begun in 1137. Ten years later, his boyhood friend—now King Louis VI—asked Suger to govern while he was away at war. For two years this peasant-born man of the Church ruled France, even putting down a rebellion against the Crown.

WHAT IS OUR HERITAGE FROM THE MIDDLE AGES?

Recent scholarship has transformed our image of the Middle Ages and given us a far better understanding of how Medieval times paved the way for the Renaissance, the Industrial Revolution and the modern era. Medieval advances in agriculture allowed Europeans to support a much larger population than before. The development of improved waterwheels and belt transmission made Europeans more productive. In the burgeoning towns of the later Middle Ages we can see the seeds of commerce, capitalism, and the middle class.

Medieval Europeans also benefited from inventions borrowed from the East—the horse harness, the stirrup, Arabic numbers, paper, gunpowder. The magnetic compass, which was invented in China, supplied the crucial counterpart for a European innovation, the fixed rudder. Together, they let sailors venture farther and more safely, setting the stage for an era of worldwide exploration. Even Europe itself—at least the vision of a unified Europe—owes its origin to the Medieval nation-building of Charlemagne.

As speakers of English, perhaps our greatest legacy from the Middle Ages is our language. It began the Medieval period as a Germanic tongue that few English speakers today would recognize. In the early Middle Ages, it absorbed new words from the Latin of the Church and from the languages of England's Viking invaders. *They*, *their*, and *them* are all Scandinavian words. The Norman conquest that began in 1066 brought many French words into the language. In the later Middle Ages, increased contact with continental Europe and North Africa introduced Italian and Arabic words into English. Modern English is truly a multicultural tongue, forged in the continual upheavals of Medieval history.

The more we learn about the Middle Ages, the more complex a time it seems. Although the period, like our own, was marked by brutality and violence, it had other important aspects, too. The endurance and ingenuity of its people made the Middle Ages, above all, a time of great beginnings.

BRAINSTORMING

Get ready, get set. . . STORM!

YOUR INTERESTS AND EXPERTISE

As a person with your own interests, talents, and hobbies, you contribute in myriad ways to your students' education. As a content-area specialist, you bring a unique perspective—and a unique set of needs—to your team and to the planning of a project. On these pages, you'll think about the unit from the perspective of your own discipline and from the perspective of the other disciplines. You'll use this information to communicate to your team members what goes on in your classes so that you can, as a team, interrelate your subjects and your teaching.

"SEE" WHAT IT'S ALL ABOUT

When you think about a topic from the perspective of your own discipline, it's as if you're wearing special glasses—the topic has a sharper focus. When you consider a topic from an interdisciplinary perspective, you see a topic from many angles. It's almost like wearing 3-D glasses!

Both perspectives are valuable (and necessary), but in order to see from an interdisciplinary perspective, you first need to "see" through each discipline's glasses. The web below shows how this works.

It shows how several disciplines might view baseball. Activities, questions, and thoughts sparked by the topic of baseball are listed in the language of each discipline. The arrows show some possible connections that can be made among the disciplines. Only after each subject has been considered can you see these natural connections—the foundation for an interdisciplinary exploration.

English/Literature

Make a glossary of baseball terms.
Write a biography of a baseball great.
Debate the issue of baseball as a national pastime.
Write a description of a baseball game for someone who's never seen one.

Math

Diagram a baseball field.
Explain how to interpret a baseball box score.
Demonstrate how to calculate a player's batting average.
Graph the salaries of baseball players over the past forty years.

BASEBALL

Science

What is the composition of a baseball?
How does Bernoulli's principle explain how a pitcher can throw a curve ball?
What injuries most commonly plague baseball players?
How have medical advances helped prolong the careers of some ball players?

Social Studies

Write a research report on the history of baseball.
How did the Civil War help spread baseball through the country?
Who was the first African-American player in major league baseball?
How did World War II affect baseball?

Now try this brainstorming activity with the topic of the Middle Ages.. Use the reproducible web below to brainstorm the needs, curricular objectives, and activities for each discipline. (You'll probably have more for your own discipline, but try the others, too. You may be surprised!)

After you've brainstormed, review your web, sketching the natural connections among the disciplines. Bring your "connected web" to the team meeting (pages 28-30) to share with your team members.

YOUR STUDENTS' INTERESTS AND NEEDS

The more immersed a student is in a learning activity, the more meaningful that activity becomes for him or her. Likewise, the more you involve students in the planning and development of a unit, the more they will invest of themselves in carrying it out. On these two pages, you'll brainstorm, examine, and prioritize the needs and interests of your students.

GATHER INFORMATION

You already know a lot about your kids. How can you find out more? Here are several ideas:

1. Tune in. Observe your students closely, both in and out of class. What are they talking about? What are some of their everyday concerns? What are their ethical values? What codes of behavior do they seem to live by—or admire in others? Who are their heroes? How do they respond to major news events? Do they question how these events might relate to their own lives? Are they able to empathize with others who may not be so fortunate as they? As students explore what life was like in another era, it's important for them to try to make connections between that time and now. Just as their lives have been impacted by those who have gone before, students will have the opportunity to influence future generations. Their view of the world will have an impact on what that world is to become.

2. Be a detective. Investigate students' interests and abilities. Give special-needs students some extra thought. How might they make valuable contributions to the unit? There are so many hands-on activities and projects in this unit! Who might help with the physical aspects of recreating the environment of the Middle Ages? Are there family members who might assist with such things as making costumes or constructing props? Is there anyone who might help with any videotaping you'd like done during the unit?

3. Go to the source. Ask students themselves. Here are several ways to get their input:

■ **Whole-Team Meeting:** Gather your entire team—students and teachers—for a brief team meeting. At this meeting, describe the unit topic (The Middle Ages), explaining that you're in the initial planning stages. Establish some ground rules for the meeting—for example, you don't want to get bogged down in details such as deadlines, grades, and format of student projects—and a tentative time frame for the unit. Then invite questions and suggestions. Encourage students to identify specific issues, categories of change, or problems they would like to investigate. You can use this information to determine the parameters of your unit.

■ **Interdisciplinary Brainstorming:** If you found it helpful to consider the unit from the perspective of all the disciplines, odds are that your kids will, too! Use the web on page 23 with students. Use a similar web after the unit to assess their learning!

■ **K-W-L Chart:** Use a K-W-L chart (a 3-column chart with these headings: What We Know, What We Want to Learn, What We Learned) before you begin the unit to assess prior knowledge of the historical period and to set learning goals. Use it afterwards to assess how well students met their goals. (See page 117 in the Team Tools section.)

BRAINSTORM!

Take some time to record the information you've gathered about your students.

Things to Think About

STUDENT NEEDS

✔ students' different learning styles

✔ curricular/content goals

✔ critical thinking skills

✔ affective goals

✔ special needs of supported-education students

STUDENT INTERESTS

✔ issues kids identify with

✔ activities students like best

✔ cooperative grouping

YOUR SCHOOL AND COMMUNITY RESOURCES

Carrying out an interdisciplinary unit successfully requires three key skills: (1) resourcefulness in identifying key people; (2) efficiency in locating useful materials; and (3) boldness in asking for the use of people's time and materials. On these pages, you'll brainstorm human and material resources that will help you develop and carry out a rich unit.

IDENTIFY KEY PEOPLE

The most important resource is people: other teachers and school staff members, parents, community members, and the students themselves. Our first priority was to use as many people as possible connected with the school and our teams, so we polled the faculty for any way they could tie into the unit.

Media staff can be a big help by creating and maintaining a community resources file, with names, addresses, and telephone numbers of people who are willing to serve as resources of one kind or another or as chaperones for field trips.

In Sarasota, we are very fortunate to have an annual Medieval fair, which is sponsored by the Ringling Museum of Art. Sometimes we attend the fair with students as a way to motivate them to want to learn more about this exciting period of history. More often, we attend the fair after we have put on our own version of a Medieval fair. Other communities also have fairs or festivals that celebrate life in a by-gone era. If your community has such an activity, don't miss the opportunity to tap into an important resource. Even if you can't attend with your students, you may be able to get

the names of people who can help you plan and execute your own culminating experience.

TRACK DOWN YOUR MATERIALS

Materials from all media—books, periodicals, primary-source materials, videotapes, computer data banks, films, cassettes, models, maps, posters—are also a key factor in the success of such an interdisciplinary unit. These materials help create an authentic environment in which to explore a topic, provide raw material for students to interpret and draw on, and address different learning styles. They also help get students turned on! Your media center is the center of the action during an interdisciplinary unit.

SPREAD THE WORD

The most effective method of finding unusual resources is as simple as this: Ask! People love to share. Ask media specialists and other staff members in your school who might have personal experiences, insights, or talents to share with your team. Talk to people outside of school, too—at the bookstore, clubs you belong to, the local Welcome Wagon, even the grocery store. Word travels fast.

BRAINSTORM!

Take some time to brainstorm and record all the people, places, and materials you might be able to use in this unit.

WHO

WHAT

WHERE

Things to Think About

✔ librarians and media specialists

✔ parents, relatives, PTA or PTO

✔ teachers and staff members

✔ museum guides or docents

✔ participants in Medieval fairs

✔ books (check out the Bibliography in the Student Project Book, as well as the one on pages 119-120 of this guide)

✔ videos, films, filmstrips

✔ vertical file

✔ visuals

✔ museums

✔ local libraries

TEAM MEETING

WHAT ARE OUR "BEST BETS" FOR THIS UNIT?

You've considered your own interests and expertise, your students' interests and needs, and the resources of your school and community. Now it's time to meet with your team to decide on the direction you'd like the unit to take. The reproducible form on the next page may help you reach a consensus.

TEAM MEETING Tips

✔ Consider assuming roles: recorder, leader, summarizer, clarifier, etc. This helps each team member to become involved and to stay focused during the meeting.

✔ The recorder might use chart paper or a white board to trap group ideas and decisions. Recording such information allows each team member to react and agree upon each idea. We like to photograph large charts and webs for future reference.

✔ Reaching a consensus requires time, energy, and a commitment to put the goals of the unit before individual preferences.

1 CURRICULAR GOALS
Now is the time to let your individual expertise shine. Team members depend on your input to determine the curricular goals that fit into this unit best.

2 SCHEDULING
Look for the best time based on the sequence of your curriculum. Also check your school's master calendar to avoid conflicts.

3 OUTSIDE SUPPORT
You might want to include exploratory and other key staff members in your team meetings to get their input.

4 RESPONSIBILITIES
Determine which tasks and decisions require group input and which are most effectively carried out by individual team members. Because planning time is at a premium, consider dividing up general categories of tasks (phone calls, library research, etc.) among yourselves. Then you'll just need to check in about the status of the tasks at team meetings.

1 **Which of our curricular goals best fit into this unit?**

SCIENCE: SOCIAL STUDIES:

MATH: ENGLISH/LITERATURE:

2 **What looks like the best time of year for this unit?**

3 **Who in our school and community might best be able to support our unit?**

4 **Who will be responsible for contacting resource people? Gathering resources?**

NAME: WILL CONTACT/GATHER: BY WHEN:

TEAM MEETING

NEXT TEAM MEETING

Establish a basic working routine for your team meetings so that minimal time is spent on logistics. Try to meet in the same place and/or time. Having an agenda also makes every minute of your time count. (Interesting snacks are a nice incentive, too.) The reproducible form on this page can help you set your individual and team priorities. (This form also appears in Team Tools, page 115.)

GOAL
At your next meeting, you may want to choose specific activities for the unit. Organize these activities according to time, objectives, and outcomes. (See Customizing, pages 31-46.)

ASSIGNMENTS
On your own, work through Customizing, pages 31-46 to choose the launch, instructional, and culminating activities that match your "best bets."

TEAM MEETING
Date

Time

Place

OUR GOAL FOR THE MEETING

TASKS TO DO BEFORE THE MEETING

1

2

3

4

5

CUSTOMIZING
THE UNIT

Here's how the unit can work for you!

CULMINATING EXPERIENCES

Now that you have brainstormed your interests and needs, what's next? We suggest you select a culminating experience—a powerful activity that will bring home the meaning of your unit. We found it helpful to think about this first. If you know where you're going, it's easier to figure out how to get there! This a great time to brainstorm with your team and decide which activity best suits your needs and goals. Choose from the list below or use it as a springboard for developing an original culminating activity of your own.

A MEDIEVAL FAIR: Simulation
(Activity Bank, pages 86-90)

A Medieval Fair is a great way for your classes to celebrate their knowledge of the Middle Ages while giving each student a chance to show off his or her special skill. The idea is to simulate the many trading activities and games of a real Medieval fair. Your "fair grounds" can be either indoors or outdoors. Your booths can be elaborate and custom-made or as simple as a row of tables borrowed from the cafeteria. Either way, we've suggested a broad range of games and activities, and you and your classes can come up with others of your own. To make things more realistic, students can don Medieval costumes and, for a few hours, become the Medieval people they've been studying about. It's a chance to put hands-on learning to work and have fun doing it.

MEDIEVAL TIMES: A Mini-Museum
(Activity Bank, page 91)

Like most of us, students thrive on feedback. A mini-museum lets students showcase the projects they have done for the unit and get other people's reactions to them. Students may have made simulated Medieval tools or a knight's sword and lance. They may have created scale models of a Medieval manor, a castle, or a town. They may have even produced an audiotape or a videotape about a Medieval topic. All of these can go on display. In addition, students can make exhibits specifically for the museum--maps, charts, or models--and stage dramatic re-enactments of real or imagined events. Students may even want to prepare a catalog that lists and describes the exhibits. A mini-museum lets students "publish" their work so that other students and parents can see and enjoy it.

MEDIEVAL TALES: Putting on a Pageant
(Activity Bank, page 92)

This is a simple culminating experience, but one that many students will have fun doing. Nearly anything that students like to do can be incorporated into the pageant—everything from singing, acting, and playing a musical instrument to tumbling, juggling, and other acrobatics. The activity builds on the story-telling activities on pages 18-21 of the Student Project Book.

A MEDIEVAL TAPESTRY
(Activity Bank, page 93)

In Medieval times, most people could not read, and much important information was expressed in visual terms. The stained glass windows of Medieval cathedrals have been described as a visual "Bible" designed to educate the illiterate. Another important visual medium was the tapestry. Tapestries were designed for both churches and for the homes of the nobility and depicted a wide range of subjects—not only religious ones but also figures from mythology and scenes of everyday life. This activity invites your students to design and make a paper tapestry using inexpensive materials.

UTOPIA: Imagining a Better World
(Activity Bank, page 96)

People throughout history have dreamed of making a better world. But the term *Utopia* was not used until 1516, when Sir Thomas More published a book with that title. (The word is Greek for "nowhere land.") More imagined a world where property was owned communally, where women and men were equal, and where there was complete freedom of belief. What kind of world would your students like to create? This activity gives them a chance to grapple with that question—and you may be surprised by their answers.

For ideas about other culminating experiences, see "Additional Projects" on page 37.

STUDENT PROJECT AND INSTRUCTIONAL ACTIVITIES

Now that you have an idea of where you'd like your units to go, how will you get there? Look over your activity choices. Dozens of activities are described on the next few pages—and you'll probably think of plenty of your own! As you review these activities, keep in mind that many can be used in several ways. We also suggest the objectives you might emphasize with each activity, but, of course, you can customize these activities to suit your own needs.

KEY

Eng: Language Arts (English, Literature); **Math**: Mathematics; **Sci**: Science; **SS**: Social Studies

Q1: WHO WERE THE PEOPLE OF THE MIDDLE AGES?

Q2: HOW WAS MEDIEVAL SOCIETY ORGANIZED?

Q3: WHAT WAS DAILY LIFE LIKE THEN?

Q4: WHAT VALUES AND IDEAS WERE IMPORTANT IN MEDIEVAL CULTURE?

Q5: HOW DID PEOPLE IN THE MIDDLE AGES HELP SHAPE OUR WORLD TODAY?

ACTIVITY	WHEN YOU CAN USE IT	OBJECTIVES AND CURRICULUM CONNECTIONS
Once in Olde England: A Canterbury Tale **page 48**	*Launch	Introduction to The Middle Ages
The Middle Ages on Film **page 49**	*Launch	Introduction to The Middle Ages
Joan of Arc: A Woman for All Seasons **page 50**	*Launch	Introduction to The Middle Ages
The Luck of the Draw **page 51**	*Launch	Introduction to The Middle Ages
Introducing the Unit **page 52**	*Launch	Introduction to the topic
Guiding Questions **page 54**	*Launch	Preview of the course of study
Student Project: Choosing a Name **page 54**	*Q1, Q2, Q5	**SS:** use time line; do research; relate past to present
What's in a Surname? Making Decisions **page 55**	*Q1, Q2, Q5	**SS:** do research; make decisions **Eng:** write explanatory paragraphs; create directory
Student Project: Defining a Historical Role **page 56**	Q1, *Q2, *Q3	**SS:** do research; compare past and present
Trademarks: Interpreting Graphic Symbols **page 57**	*Q1, Q2, *Q3, Q5	**SS:** explore origins of trademarks; relate past to present **Eng:** interpret graphic symbols **Art:** replicate and design trademarks

ACTIVITY	WHEN YOU CAN USE IT	OBJECTIVES AND CURRICULUM CONNECTIONS
Guilds: Researching and Reporting **page 58**	Q1, *Q2, Q3, Q5	**SS**: do research; report; compare/contrast **Eng**: present oral reports; role play; write journal entries
Calculating the Medieval Way **pages 59-60**	Q1, *Q3	**Math**: use Roman numerals; calculate; use non-standard algorithms **SS**: explore numeration systems; relate past to present
The Coin of the Realm: Exchanging Currency **page 61**	Q1, Q3, *Q5	**Math**: compare/contrast currencies; exchange currencies **SS**: do research **Eng**: participate in simulations
Diet: Preparing a Medieval Menu **page 62**	*Q1, *Q3	**SS**: do research; construct charts **Sci**: compare/contrast diets
Herbs: Growing Your Own **page 63**	Q1, *Q3, Q5	**SS**: do research; trace origins of herbs **Sci**: investigate medicinal uses; grow herb garden
Feasts: "Hosting" a Medieval Banquet **page 64**	Q1, Q2, Q3, *Q4	**SS**: do research; compare/contrast **Math**: make scale drawings/diagrams **Eng**: role play **Sci**: prepare menus
Student Project: Facts and Feelings **page 65**	*Q4	**SS**: do research; compare past and present **Eng**: synthesize research; write essays
Code of Behavior: Graphing Good Deeds **page 66**	Q1, Q2, *Q4, *Q5	**SS**: do research **Math**: graph data
Heraldry: Designing Coats of Arms **pages 67-68**	Q1, Q3, *Q4	**SS**: do research; relate past to present **Eng**: interpret symbols **Art**: create symbols
Heroes: Responding to Literature **page 69**	*Q1, Q4	**SS**: identify heroes/heroic qualities **Eng**:read fiction/nonfiction; compose poetry **Art**: design medals
The Best Policy: Journal Writing **page 70**	*Q4	**Eng**: interpret idioms; write journal entries; explore word/phrase origins; brainstorm lists
Student Project: Where Do I Dwell? **page 71**	Q1, *Q3	**SS**: do research
Towns: Creating Scale Models **page 72**	Q1, Q2, *Q3	**SS**: do research; construct replica of Medieval town **Math**: apply scale measurement
Castle: Designing Your Own **pages 73-74**	Q1, *Q3	**SS**: do research **Math**: create scale models/drawings

ACTIVITY	WHEN YOU CAN USE IT	OBJECTIVES AND CURRICULUM CONNECTIONS
Student Project: An Ordinary Day page 75	Q1, *Q3, *Q5	**SS:** do research; analyze cause-effect relationships **Eng:** write journal entries; write monologues
Listening to Medieval Music page 76	*Q4, *Q5	**Eng:** compare/contrast; write music reviews **Music:** identify features of musical work
Student Project: My Medieval Story page 77	Q1, *Q2, *Q3	**SS:** do research **Eng:** synthesize information; make notes for narratives
Writing, Medieval Style page 78	Q1, *Q3	**Eng:** write letters/invitations **Sci:** research writing substances
The Vikings Are Coming! Recreating an Event page 79	Q1, *Q3	**SS:** do research; trace routes on maps; propose solutions to problems; think critically/creatively **Eng:** compose poetry; read/report on Viking literature
The Crusades: Researching and Reporting page 80	Q1, *Q3, *Q4	**SS:** do research and report; read and make maps
The Black Death: Analyzing Its Impact page 81	Q1, *Q3	**SS:** do research; interpret maps/charts; identify cause/effect; relate past to present **Eng:** brainstorm solutions to problems; write paragraphs
Rediscovering Medieval Women page 82	Q1, Q3, Q4, *Q5	**SS:** analyze gender discrimination; relate past to present **Eng:** write biographical sketches
Student Project: Planning a Presentation	*Q1, Q2, Q3	**SS:** do research; analyze cause and effect **Eng:** plan presentations; write narratives
The Play's the Thing! Dramatizations page 84	Q1, Q3, *Q4, Q5	**Eng:** read/discuss Medieval tales; present dramatic interpretations
A Medieval Fair: Simulation pages 86-90	*Culmination	Celebration of Success
Medieval Times: A Mini-Museum page 91	*Culmination	Celebration of Success
Medieval Tales: Putting on a Pageant page 92	*Culmination	Celebration of Success
A Medieval Tapestry page 93	*Culmination	Celebration of Success
Utopia: Imagining a Better World page 94	*Culmination	Celebration of Success

ADDITIONAL PROJECTS AND ACTIVITIES

What makes this Medieval unit so successful is the fact that there are innumerable ways to tie exploratory and advisory classes with the academic material. The following activities are some possibilities for connecting!

MUSIC
- Listen to recordings of Medieval music.
- Research the origins of Medieval music.

PERFORMING ENSEMBLES
- Choral and instrumental ensembles may take part in any of the culminating experiences, either to provide a concert of Medieval music or to accompany a dramatic presentation.

ART
- Draw pictures of real or imaginary Medieval events.
- Create masks for a Medieval play or pageant.
- Draw a cross-section of a cathedral.
- Design a poster about the Crusades that includes a map and portraits of some important Crusaders.

HOME ECONOMICS
- Prepare a kind of food commonly eaten during the Middle Ages (see Bibliography for research ideas).
- Make a chart that compares and contrasts Medieval and modern clothes in terms of materials used to make them, colors, and durability.
- Make a chart that compares Medieval and modern diets, dividing the foods of both times into proteins, carbohydrates, and fats, and drawing conclusions about which one provides more balanced nutrition.

TECHNICAL ARTS
- Create a video about a Medieval topic.
- Research one of the technological advances made during the Middle Ages, such as the magnetic compass, papermaking, and water power (see Bibliography for research ideas).

- Learn about the building techniques used in Medieval cathedrals.
- Build a papier-mâché model of a cathedral or a castle.

FOREIGN LANGUAGES
- Students with a knowledge of Spanish can translate a brief passage from Cervantes or another Spanish writer of the Middle Ages and present it to the class in both Spanish and English. (The same activity can also be done by students with a knowledge of French or Italian, using the work of Christine de Pisan or Dante.)

COMPUTERS
- Design a coat of arms.
- Create a data base about the Middle Ages.
- Create graphics--circle graphs, time lines, etc.-- about Medieval topics for a mini-museum (one of the culminating experiences).

PHYSICAL EDUCATION
- Research the training techniques of a Medieval knight and simulate some of them..
- Get a sense of what overland travel was like in Medieval times by taking a day-long walk, stopping to eat and rest whenever necessary.
- Play a soccer game "Medieval style"--with as many people on each of the two teams as are available. (In the Middle Ages, a soccer team sometimes included all of a town's residents!)

ADVISORY
- Set time aside when students can meet with students in the grade above who did the unit last year. Students love to be able to impart information, rather than receiving it, and the younger students will benefit greatly from learning what worked and what did not.

LAUNCH ACTIVITIES

The launch is the students' first exposure to the unit, so it needs to be a real "grabber." Choose wisely because it creates a mind-set for the entire unit. The activities you select could be for a large group (your whole team), individual class activities, or a combination of both. You know your students! Choose whatever you think will make the best "hook" for your particular population.

ONCE IN OLDE ENGLAND:
A Canterbury Tale
(Activity Bank, page 48)

Barbara Cohen's contemporary retelling of four stories from Chaucer in her book, *Canterbury Tales*, makes a fascinating introduction to the Medieval world. We suggest you choose one and read it aloud to the class. The stories include "The Nun's Priest's Tale," "The Pardoner's Tale," "The Wife of Bath's Tale," and "The Franklin's Tale," each of which can be read in 15 or 20 minutes, leaving ample time for an introduction and for class discussion. Cohen captures the appeal of Chaucer's down-to-earth storytelling, and his insights into human nature are as apt today as ever. You also might want to borrow a library recording of Chaucer's own words in Middle English to play for the class. At first it may sound like a foreign language, but, by following along with a printed text, both you and students will be surprised how much you can understand.

THE MIDDLE AGES ON FILM
(Activity Bank, page 49)

Most of what your students already know about the Middle Ages probably comes from films. Watching a film set in the Middle Ages as a class gives you a chance to launch the unit in an entertaining way, while preparing students to compare the cinematic view of the Medieval world with the historians'

view—which they will learn about in the unit. If your schedule prohibits seeing an entire film, you might preview one of the films listed and choose a representative scene to watch together.

JOAN OF ARC: A Woman for All Seasons
(Activity Bank, page 50)

For 92 years France and England battle one another in a conflict that seems endless. Suddenly a new French commander breaks the stalemate, and that leader turns out to be a 17-year-old girl! No wonder Joan of Arc has caught the world's imagination for five centuries. This activity uses the life of one extraordinary hero to get your students "hooked" on the Middle Ages.

LUCK OF THE DRAW
(Activity Bank, page 51)

We devised this activity to solve one problem we had with our Medieval unit: everyone wanted to be part of the nobility. We found that using a lottery to choose each student's Medieval role was a quick and easy solution to the problem. This activity, which only needs to take a few minutes, can be combined with any of the other launches, if you wish.

ADDITIONAL IDEAS

READ ALOUD

Barbara Cohen's *Canterbury Tales* (described above) is just one of the many Medieval readings available for this age group. If your students enjoy being read to, you might consider reading a selection from one of the books listed in the Bibliography of the Student Project Book or from the additional books listed on pages 119-120.

GUEST SPEAKER

Inviting a guest speaker can be a stimulating introduction to a unit, and there are several ways of finding speakers with a knowledge of the Middle Ages. You might invite a professor or even a graduate student who studies Medieval history, literature, or art at a local college or university. If a local university, museum, or library has a Medieval collection, you might ask its curator to speak to your classes. Whoever the speaker is, we suggest that you work with them to select a specific topic with strong student appeal, such as The Crusades or Joan of Arc.

CLASSROOM CONCERT

You might invite a local musician to perform some Medieval music for you classes. If this launch appeals to you but you cannot find a musician, you can use recorded music instead. "Listening to Medieval Music" on page 76 will give you some ideas about how to structure this launch.

TEAM MEETING

WHAT IS THE SCOPE OF OUR UNIT? THE SEQUENCE?

By now you've reviewed the activities and considered which you prefer. Get together with your team to agree upon the specific activities you'll do and the order in which you'll do them. The reproducible form on the next page can help you organize your thoughts. After you've reached a consensus, record your decisions on the Unit Curriculum Planner, Team Tools, pages 104-105. Make sure each team member has a copy.

1 CULMINATING CONSIDERATIONS
How much space is available? Can your facility hold all students plus parents and other volunteers?

2 ACTIVITY SELECTION
Will you cover all the Guiding Questions in your unit? How will this affect your selection of activities?

3 THE "FUN" FACTOR
Do the activities that excite you! Your enthusiasm will be contagious!
Which activities will the exploratory and resource staff be involved with?
Use the Objectives Checklist (Team Tools, page 110) to be sure your instructional goals are met.

4 STUDENT PROJECT
Will each team member participate in managing and evaluating the student project? Or will just one member be responsible for it? If so, who?

5 LAUNCH
Will your launch involve the whole team? Or individual classes? Do you have the facilities for this?

1 **What do we want to do as a culminating experience?**

2 **Which are the instructional activities that lead up to the culminating experience?**

SCIENCE: SOCIAL STUDIES:

MATH: ENGLISH/LITERATURE:

3 **What other instructional activities do we really want to do?**

4 **How do we want to handle the student project?**

5 **How will we launch our unit?**

TEAM MEETING

WHEN WILL WE SCHEDULE OUR UNIT?

Once you know the *what*, the *when* is easy. Use the reproducible form on the next page to determine the time frame of your unit and to consider the logistics involved. Record your decisions on the Unit Schedule (Team Tools, page 106). Distribute copies of this calendar to everyone involved, especially the exploratory teachers. This will give them a chance to see where they can help out.

1 TIMING CONSIDERATIONS
How much time *do* you want to spend on the unit? How much time *do* you have? Remember that some culminating activities require as much preparation as the unit itself.

2 STAFF INVOLVEMENT
When you schedule, include all academic teachers who will be directly involved, as well as representatives from the exploratory teachers who will be involved. Better yet, include all teachers who will be involved. Offer lots of suggestions, but let them choose how they best fit in.

3 FLEXIBILITY
Think about when you'll need flexible blocks of time for films, guest speakers, etc. Will there be other occasions when you'll want to group students differently for instruction?

4 CHECKPOINTS
Commit to your checkpoints at the beginning, and make them happen! They'll help you avoid a common problem in interdisciplinary units—the dreaded "black hole" in the middle of your unit.

5 NON-ACADEMIC TIME
If you have an advisory or home-base period, take advantage of the time to check up on student progress with projects and other activities. You might also use the time to discuss difficult issues students may encounter in their research.

1 *How long will our unit be? What will our begin/end dates be?*

2 *Who do we need to include in the scheduling process?*

3 *When will we need flexible blocks of time?*

4 *When will we schedule checkpoints for ourselves during the unit?*

5 *How will we use the TAP/advisory/home-base period?*

TEAM MEETING

HOW WILL WE MANAGE THE UNIT?

Congratulations! You've made some big decisions about your unit. Now consider all the details that guarantee the success of your unit—responsibilities, lesson plans, resources, and evaluation. We've provided several different forms to record your plans. (See Team Tools, pages 106-109.) Use whichever is most comfortable for you.

KEY DECISIONS

How will you determine the selection of student projects? Will students choose for themselves? Will you guide their selection? If so, to what extent?

What are your expectations for students? How will you evaluate? (See pages 95-102 of the Team Planning Guide.)

How can you help students be successful?

- To involve students in planning and management of the unit, use the **Unit Schedule**, page 106.

- To help students stay focused, post the **Guiding Questions** in each team member's classroom.

KEY RESPONSIBILITIES

Who will manage the student project?

Who will locate, gather, and follow up on resource people?

Who will be responsible for any special preparations your culminating experience might require?

OUR TEAM'S ACTIVITY PLAN

By now you might be curious about what we actually did! We spent two weeks on the unit. Our plans appear on pages 45-46.

Communication is important for a successful IDU. Grade-level and team meetings prior to and during the unit are essential.

Overlap among Guiding Questions and classes is just fine! The questions help you plan the unit and help the kids understand the unit's scope—they guide the unit, but they don't drive it.

Activity Plan

WEEK 1 (Student Project Book)	MONDAY	TUESDAY	WEDNESDAY	THURSDAY	FRIDAY
SOCIAL STUDIES	Immersion Day	What's in a Surname p. 55 — SPB pp. 6-9	Guilds p. 58 — SPB pp. 10-11	Where Do I Dwell? — SPB pp. 14-15	Rediscovering Medieval Women p. 82
ENGLISH		Writing exploratory paragraphs		SPB pp. 12-13	Read essays
LITERATURE	Read a Canterbury Tale p. 48	Listen to Chaucer recording			Excerpt from Queen Eleanor
MATH	Calculating the Medieval Way p. 59 →		Scale drawings	Coin of the Realm p. 61 →	
SCIENCE		Diet p. 62 →	→		Herbs p. 63
TAP/Advisory	SPB pp. 4-5		BEGIN STUDENT PROJECTS!	Work on projects →	
OTHERS	Physical Fitness →|			→|

Activity Plan

WEEK 2	MONDAY	TUESDAY	WEDNESDAY	THURSDAY	FRIDAY
SOCIAL STUDIES	Using a Time Line — SPB pp.28-29	Research techniques	The Black Death p. 81	Who Was Robin Hood?	Medieval Fair p. 86 →
ENGLISH	Write a journal entry — SPB p. 16-17	My Medieval Story — SPB pp.18-19		Class Presentations — SPB pp. 20-21	
LITERATURE	SPB p. 34-37		Excerpt from *Travels of Marco Polo*		
MATH	Graphing Good Deeds p. 66 →				
SCIENCE	Vaulted ceilings — SPB pp.38-39	Writing Medieval Style p. 78	The Black Death p. 81		
TAP/Advisory	Work on projects →				Evaluation — SPB pp. 22
OTHERS	Listening to Medieval Music p. 76		Designing Coats of Arms pp. 67-68 →		

Student Project Book

ACTIVITY
BANK

ACTIVITIES–the heart of any unit!

ONCE IN OLDE ENGLAND: A CANTERBURY TALE

This launch introduces students to Medieval life through the work of one of England's finest writers, Geoffrey Chaucer. This version of his Canterbury Tales, recast in contemporary language, makes Chaucer's stories accessible to American students.

When You Can Use It
★Launch

Objectives
■ to introduce the unit

Materials and Resources
■ *Canterbury Tales*, selected, translated, and adapted by Barbara Cohen and illustrated by Trina Schart Hyman (Morrow, 1988)

HOW TO GO ABOUT IT

Beforehand
Choose one of the four Canterbury tales adapted by Barbara Cohen that will most appeal to your students.

1. Explain the background of the story to the class. It was written in the late 1300s by the English writer Geoffrey Chaucer. Chaucer's book *The Canterbury Tales* describes a group of people who take a fifty-mile journey from London to the city of Canterbury, the site of one of England's most beautiful churches. The trip takes many days, and each night the pilgrims tell one another stories to pass the time. This is one of those tales.

2. Read the story to the class and ask students to comment on it. What did they like or dislike about it? How would they describe the person who told the story? What did they learn about life in the 1300s?

3. Chaucer's book was written in an earlier form of English called Middle English. Explain to students that the English language has changed so much during the last 600 years that Chaucer's words have to be translated into modern English before we know exactly what he's saying. You may, however, want to play a brief passage from an audio-cassette of the *Tales* in their original form. You and your students may both be surprised at how much of Middle English you can understand if you follow along with a modern translation. There are bilingual paperback editions available that are especially helpful for this purpose. Many libraries have Chaucer recordings in their collections. See Bibliography for details.

THE MIDDLE AGES ON FILM

Hollywood—and other film makers around the world—have long been attracted to the Middle Ages. And, whether the man wielding the sword was Errol Flynn or Kevin Costner, Medieval tales have been popular with film audiences. This activity uses the evocative power of film to get your students "hooked" on the Middle Ages.

When You Can Use It
★Launch

Objective
■ to introduce the unit

Materials and Resources
■ One of the many films set during Medieval times. Three good choices are:

Brother Sun, Sister Moon
The Lion in Winter
Robin Hood

See Bibliography for details.

HOW TO GO ABOUT IT

1. These films are available in many local video stores. (If your school or district has a policy on the showing of rental videos, be sure to comply with it.) Choose one and present it to your class in more than one session, so that you will have time for discussion in the second. You might want to have all the classes that are particpating in the unit view the film as a group, because film viewing is more fun that way. Use a large screen televsion for the viewing, if your school has one.

2. Ask students to comment on the film. The following questions can be used to guide the student discussion.

■ Did you like or dislike the film? Why?

■ Where does the film's action take place?

■ Is there any way to tell *when* the action takes place (or at least in what century)?

■ What did you learn about the period from the movie?

■ What do you want to know more about?

3. Invite students to think about the time and place in which the story was set. Could the same story be set in modern times? What is special about the period in which the events occurred?

JOAN OF ARC: A WOMAN FOR ALL SEASONS

Joan of Arc is one of history's most fascinating figures. At a time when women were given few chances to take part in public life, she not only became a military leader at the age of 17 but turned the tide in a war between France and England that had been going on for generations. This launch activity will introduce your students to an unforgettable woman.

When You Can Use It
★Launch

Objective
■ to introduce the unit

Materials and Resources
■ Encyclopedias and other reference books
■ *Beyond the Myth: The Story of Joan of Arc* by Polly S. Brooks (Harper Collins, 1990)

■ *Joan of Arc* by Susan Banfield (Chelsea House, 1985)
■ *Joan of Arc: Soldier Saint* by Tracy Christopher (Chelsea House, 1993)
■ *Young Joan* (fiction) by Barbara Dana (Harper Collins, 1991)

HOW TO GO ABOUT IT

1. Ask students if they have ever heard of Joan of Arc. Who was she? When and where did she live? Why is she famous?

2. Provide students with enough information about the life of Joan of Arc to get them interested. She was born in eastern France about 1412. France and England had then been at war for 75 years, and English troops occupied much of France. As a teenager, Joan worked spinning wool into yarn, but one day, while she was working, she heard a voice telling her that she must help King Charles of France to defeat the English. At first, Joan doubted the voice, but eventually she believed that the voice came

from God and that she must obey it. The story of how she did and eventually led the men of the French army in crucial victories over the English—at the age of 17— is one of the most amazing in history.

3. Have students do research about Joan of Arc and then write biographical sketches of her. If they wish, they can also find images to accompany their sketches, either reproductions of works of art or stills from the various film versions of her life. (A new French film about her was released in 1994.) Ask students to include a statement telling why they think Joan of Arc has been such an interesting person to people throughout history.

THE LUCK OF THE DRAW

This unit asks students to adopt a Medieval role, and, left to their own devices, each student would probably like to be king or queen (wouldn't we all!). One way to avoid any conflicts about who plays which role is to assign social positions in the same way they were assigned during Medieval times: by pure chance. This launch activity will divide your class into lords and ladies, peasants and serfs, knights, clergy, merchants, and wanderers, giving each person an equal chance to win each role.

When You Can Use It
★Launch

Objective
■ to introduce the unit

Materials and Resources
■ A stack of cards corresponding to the number of students in your class.

HOW TO GO ABOUT IT

Beforehand
On each card, write a Medieval role. For a class of 40, you might divide the number of roles along these lines:

> 20—serfs
>
> 10—peasants
>
> 2—clergy (priests, monks, or nuns)
>
> 2—troubadours
>
> 2—merchants
>
> 2—knights
>
> 2—nobles (lords or ladies)

1. Tell the class that for this unit each student needs to have a Medieval role. During the Middle Ages, a person's role in society was determined chiefly by who their parents were. If a person's parents were in the nobility, that person was, too. If they were serfs, so were their children. One of the few exceptions was in the Church, which accepted both nobles and peasants to be members of the clergy, whether as priests, monks, or nuns.

2. Students' Medieval roles will be determined by choosing a card at random from a box or bag. Pass the box or bag containing the cards around the room, allowing each student to pick one.

3. When everyone has a card, you or a student should record the role of each person in the class. Girls as well as boys may take any role, including that of knight.

THE MIDDLE AGES: INTRODUCING THE UNIT

Student Project Book, pages 4 and 5

When You Can Use It
★ **Launch**

Objectives
■ to introduce the topic; to discuss students' preconceptions of the Middle Ages

MANAGEMENT TIPS

✔ Begin by asking students what they know about the following names and terms—or what people or places they associate with each one: peasant, castle, Robin Hood, knight, The Crusades, cathedral, Marco Polo.

✔ Discuss the impression students have of the Middles Ages from books, films, TV, pop songs, folk music, or other sources.

✔ Ask students to answer the following questions on the left side of a piece of paper under the heading "What I Think Now":

1. What was the most common occupation in Medieval Europe?

2. Who are three important people who lived during the Middle Ages?

3. What was the Black Death?

When the unit has been completed, students can add a new heading on the right, "What I Have Learned," and answer the questions a second time.

✔ Encourage students to see this unit as a way of testing their notions about Medieval people and their way of life.

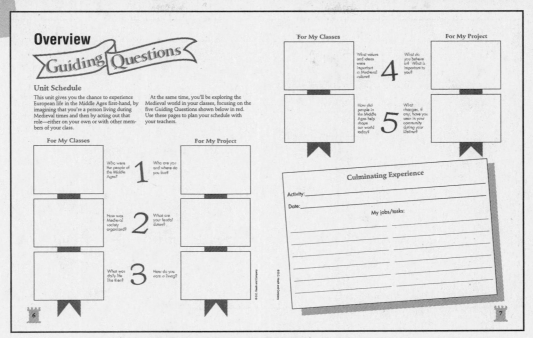

Student Project Book, pages 6 and 7

When You Can Use It
★ Launch

Objective
■ to preview the course of study

When You Can Use It
■ a copy of master unit schedule

MANAGEMENT TIPS

✔ Point out the large numerals 1 through 5. Read aloud the guiding question to the left of each numeral. Tell students that they will learn the answers to these questions in their classes. Then read aloud the corresponding question to the right of each numeral. Point out that the "you" in the column at the right refers not to them, but to the Medieval person they'll imagine themselves to be.

✔ Use your master unit schedule to tell students what they'll be doing in their classes and when. Students can record that schedule in the left-hand column. Then give students time to look over the Student Project pages and to come up with the tasks and schedule they'll follow as they work on the project. They can record those items in the right-hand column.

STUDENT PROJECT: Choosing a Name

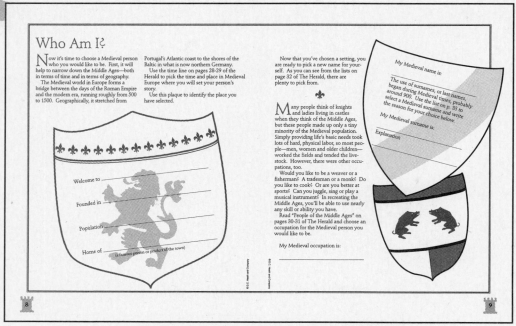

Student Project Book, pages 8 and 9

When You Can Use It

★ **Q1:** Who were the people of the Middle Ages?

Q2: How was Medieval society organized?

Q5: How did people in the Middle Ages help shape our world today?

Objectives

■ **Social Studies:** to use a time line; to conduct research; to relate past to present

Materials and Resources

■ The Herald

  Map, pages 26-27

  Time Line, pages 28-29

  People of the Middle Ages, pages 30-31

  What's in a Name, pages 32-33

■ an encyclopedia

MANAGEMENT TIPS

✔ In this activity, each student chooses a Medieval person who she or he would like to be. Depending on what Culminating Experience you're planning, you may want the class to choose people from a single place or from various places. If you're having a feast or festival, for example, the class needs to have a common setting. If you're having a fair, the people might come from a wide range of places, near and far.

✔ Be sure students understand that only the events above the time line refer to Medieval Europe. Students can also use the map on pages 26-27 of The Herald to select a Medieval place.

✔ You may want to have each student make a nametag with his or her Medieval name.

WHAT'S IN A SURNAME? MAKING DECISIONS

In early Medieval Europe, people lived in such small communities that they needed only first names. But as towns increased in size and people began to travel more, it became clear that first names were not enough. In this activity, students explore how the practice of using surnames got started in Medieval Europe, and how those surnames were chosen.

When You Can Use It
★ **Q1:** Who were the people of the Middle Ages?

Q2: How was Medieval society organized?

Q5: How did people in the Middle Ages help shape our world today?

Objectives
■ **Social Studies:** to do research; to make decisions

■ **English:** to write explanatory paragraphs; to create an alphabetized directory of names

What You Might Assess
■ inclusion of supporting statements in students' paragraphs

■ correct alphabetization in directory

Materials and Resources
■ The Herald, page 33

■ Art supplies

HOW TO GO ABOUT IT

1. Demonstrate the importance of surnames by asking students to imagine a world in which they all had only first names. Point out how confusing this situation would be! Then ask students to identify three settings in which last names, or surnames, are especially important. (Examples might include hospitals, schools, corporations, and so on.)

2. Explain that during the early Middle Ages, most people had only a single name. The use of surnames emerged around 900 AD. Direct students to page 33 of The Herald, and ask them to read about the different ways that surnames originated. Then ask them to speculate about the derivation of their own surnames. You might choose a few surnames to use as examples.

■ McDonald—son of Donald (*Mc* or *Mac* in Irish or Scottish names has the meaning "son of.")

■ Fernandez—son of Fernando (The *ez* at the end of Spanish names has the same meaning.)

■ Levy—descendant of the Levites, an Israeli tribe of temple servants

■ Chan—from a Chinese word meaning "old"

3. Ask students to examine the list of surnames in The Herald. Then encourage discussion of the surnames they have selected for their Medieval roles. Ask each student to write a paragraph explaining the reasons for his or her choice.

4. Students may enjoy making a "directory" of their Medieval names. Suggest that each student write his or her name on a slip of paper, surname first. Then have a group of students alphabetize the last names and create a composite listing. The names might be copied onto a long scroll for display in the classroom.

Extension
Encourage students to explore the origins of their own given first names and last names. Parents and other family members should be able to shed some light; there are also several books available on the origins and meanings of names.

STUDENT PROJECT: DEFINING A HISTORICAL ROLE

How Do I Do My Work?

Most Medieval occupations required only a few simple tools—a farmer's plow and hoe, a knight's sword and lance, a weaver's loom. Even the basic work of cathedral building—stone-carving—was done with little more than a hammer, a chisel, and a wedge to split the stone.

List the tools needed for your Medieval occupation. Also tell how you plan to make them.

Tools	How I'll Make Them
_____	_____
_____	_____
_____	_____
_____	_____

What's For Lunch?

People in the Middle Ages looked forward to lunch as much as we do—more so, because they worked harder physically. List the foods you might have eaten for a typical Medieval lunch and then prepare those foods and eat them for your lunch at school.

Just as today, during the Middle Ages the clothes a person wore depended largely on his or her occupation. Find an illustration that shows how you might have dressed and draw or trace a "self-portrait" in the space to the right.

Student Project Book, pages 10 and 11

When You Can Use It

Q1: Who were the people of the Middle Ages?

★ **Q2:** How was Medieval society organized?

★ **Q3:** What was daily life like then?

Objectives

- **Social Studies:** to do research; to compare past and present

Materials and Resources

- "People of the Middle Ages" in The Herald, pages 30-31
- One or more of these books for information about Medieval occupations: Giovanni Casselli's *The Middle Ages*, Sheila Sancha's *Luttrell's Village*, or, for more advanced students, Marjorie Rowling's *Life in Medieval Times*.

MANAGEMENT TIPS

✔ Students with similar roles might be grouped together for this activity. When the activity is completed, students can return to their original groups to share information. You will probably want to lead a class discussion showing students what to look for in their research. They will first have to find out what tools were used in their occupations in Medieval times. Any of the three books listed here will provide that information for most occupations. Students may also need your help in determining the relationships between the various classes of Medieval people.

✔ Have students compare and contrast a midday meal during the Middle Ages with their own school lunches.

✔ You might wish to reserve the role of "King" for the principal, the superintendent, or some other adult. In this way, when the students are planning their culminating activity, they will have the additional excitement of knowing that the "King" will be in attendance.

TRADEMARKS: INTERPRETING GRAPHIC SYMBOLS

Trademarks are names or symbols used to distinguish one maker's goods from those of another. In Medieval Europe, guild badges (which we call trademarks) were used instead of lettered signs to mark the shops of tradespeople. In this activity, students explore how the custom of using trademarks (which began in ancient times) persists today.

When You Can Use It

★ **Q1:** Who were the people of the Middle Ages?

Q2: How was Medieval society organized?

★ **Q3:** What was daily life like then?

Q5: How did people in the Middle Ages help shape our world today?

Objectives

■ **Social Studies:** to explore the origin of trademarks; to relate past to present

■ **English:** to understand the function of graphic symbols; to interpret symbols

■ **Art:** to replicate and design original trademarks

What You Might Assess

■ students' replications of contemporary trademarks

■ appropriateness of symbols in students' designs for Medieval trademarks

Materials and Resources

■ Art supplies

■ The Herald, page 33

HOW TO GO ABOUT IT

1. Share the information in the above sidenote with students. You may also want to share with them examples of a few Medieval trademarks used by wool merchants:

2. Ask the students if they can identify any trademarks on their clothing, in the classroom, in places in the community, and so forth. (As an example, you may want to draw McDonald's golden arches on the chalkboard.) If necessary, point out that a trademark identifies a product or a service. It may include a word, a sentence, a name, a symbol, or a combination of these. (The "spoken" part of a trademark is called a "brand name.")

3. Distribute art supplies, and then ask students to illustrate at least ten contemporary trademarks. These may represent any kind of company, service, business, etc. When students are done, have them share their work with classmates. Ask:

■ Which trademarks appear most frequently?

■ What does this suggest about their effectiveness as advertisements?

4. Referring students to page 33 of The Herald, ask them to design their own trademarks for the occupations listed under "Surnames." You may want to expand the list by adding the following:

■ cooper (barrel maker)

■ mason (bricklayer)

■ nail maker

■ alchemist

■ vintner (winemaker)

■ saddle maker

■ cobbler (shoemaker)

The finished products can be displayed in the classroom. Or, if a Medieval fair is planned, they can be used on individual booths.

Do not be surprised if students begin to closely scrutinize each other's clothing and belongings for trademarks. It makes for a most interesting class!

Dale

GUILDS: RESEARCHING AND REPORTING

As towns and trade grew during the Middle Ages, companies of merchants joined together to form guilds. They did so not only for their own personal safety but also to increase their profits. In this activity, students do research to find out about the importance of guilds to the social structure of the Middle Ages in Europe.

When You Can Use It

Q1: Who were the people of the Middle Ages?

★ **Q2:** How was Medieval society organized?

Q3: What was daily life like then?

Q5: How did people in the Middle Ages help shape our world today?

Objectives

■ **Social Studies:** to research and report on Medieval guilds; to compare/contrast Medieval guilds with modern trade unions

■ **English:** to present oral reports; to role play; to write journal entries

What You Might Assess

■ organization, content, and delivery of oral reports

■ creativity and accuracy of content in dramatic presentations and journal entries

Materials and Resources

■ Social studies texts

■ Encyclopedias and other reference sources

■ Pictures of guildhalls (if available)

■ *Guilds* by Neil Grant (Franklin Watts, 1972); out of print but may be available through a local library

---

HOW TO GO ABOUT IT

1. Share the information in the sidenote with students. Review with them what they may have learned about guilds from their social studies texts and other sources. Discuss the steps in becoming a guild member: apprentice, journeyman, master. Point out that on becoming a master, a guild member was permitted to open up shop and be called *Master Smith* or *Master Cooper*, titles which over time have become *Mister Smith* or *Mister Cooper*.

2. Ask students to choose some aspect of Medieval guilds about which to do more extensive research. You might list topics such as the following on the board:

■ Guilds and the Growth of Towns

■ Becoming a Guild Member: Apprentice, Journeyman, Master

■ Guilds: Rules, Regulations, and Codes of Behavior

■ Guilds and Medieval Drama

■ Guilds and Modern Trade Unions

After students have completed their research, have them present their findings in the form of oral reports.

3. As an alternative to the above, you might have students work in cooperative groups to do research about individual craft guilds and then share their findings in the form of dramatic presentations (for example, role plays). Following are just a few of the tradespeople who were organized by guilds: armorers, bakers, basket makers, bottlers, butchers, cobblers, coopers, dyers, fishmongers, jewelers, masons, millers, nail makers, pepperers, poulterers, saddlers, tailors, tanners, vintners, weavers, wool merchants.

4. Ask students who have taken on the personas of merchants or craftspeople to speculate about their experiences in joining a guild. Invite these students to write journal entries to record their progress through each of the three stages: apprentice, journeyman, master. Other students might write journal entries to describe their relationships or dealings with guild merchants or craftspeople.

Extension

If students have relatives or acquaintances who are members of a union, they might interview these people about their experiences. Have students compare and contrast Medieval guilds with modern trade unions. (Medieval guilds provided health insurance, retirement benefits, and social activities—just as today's trade unions do.)

CALCULATING THE MEDIEVAL WAY

During the Middle Ages, Roman numerals were gradually replaced by Arabic (really Hindu) numbers. In this activity, students learn first-hand how cumbersome it is to calculate with Roman numerals. They also explore some other "old" ways of multiplying.

When You Can Use It
Q1: Who were the people of the Middle Ages?
★ **Q3:** What was daily life like then?

Objectives
■ **Math:** to use Roman numerals; to make arithmetic calculations; to use non-standard algorithms
■ **Social Studies:** to explore the history of systems of numeration; to relate past to present

What You Might Assess
■ understanding of Roman numerals
■ recognition of the limitations of the Roman system in doing complex calculations
■ ability to follow the steps involved in solving algorithms using non-traditional methods

Materials and Resources
■ Chart of Roman numerals
■ Encyclopedias and other reference books

HOW TO GO ABOUT IT

1. Display a chart of Roman numerals, and review with students the value of each symbol. You might point out how some of the symbols were devised. (It is thought that X came from two V's placed together, and that L came from the shape formed by the first finger and thumb held at right angles to each other.) Have students use Roman numerals to write such things as their ages, the current year, the years in which they were born in their Medieval roles.

2. Ask students to speculate why mathematical calculations became more and more important as trade increased. Challenge them to add and subtract using these numbers. For example:

XLVI + XXXII = ?

CCIX - LVIII = ?

Encourage students to describe their feelings as they try to calculate with these numbers. Then change the "+" and "-" signs to "x," and ask students to multiply the numbers. Can they meet the challenge? (We like to take this opportunity to talk about how much easier the Hindu-Arabic system is to use, and just how handy zero is!)

3. Tell students that with the introduction of the Hindu-Arabic numeration system, multiplication became possible to perform without counters. One method, called "peasant multi-plication," was more likely used by merchants (peasants in the Middle Ages needed to do little multiplying). Demonstrate "peasant multiplication" for students.

■ Make a chart. Place the two numbers to be multiplied at the top.

■ Double the number on the left. Write the new number below.

■ Halve the number on the right. Ignoring any remainder, write the new number below.

■ Continue doubling and halving until the number on the right side is 1.

■ Cross out any line in which the number on the right side is an even number.

■ Add any remaining answers on the left side (those opposite odd numbers).

33	x 68
~~66~~	~~34~~
132	17
~~264~~	~~8~~
~~528~~	~~4~~
~~1056~~	~~2~~
2112	1

132 + 2112 = 2244

Invite students to use "peasant multiplication" to find other products. They might work in pairs to provide each other with factors to be multiplied and to check answers.

4. Tell students that another method of multiplication, more closely related to the one we use today, comes from the writings of an Arab named al-Khwarizmi. The earliest known explanations of operations with decimal numbers are contained in these writings. Use the following example to demonstrate:

563 x 731 = ?

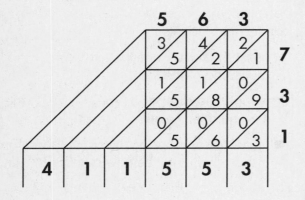

- Make a grid corresponding to the number of digits in the two factors. (For two three-digit numbers, you need a grid of nine squares.)
- Write one factor across the top; write the other down the right side.
- Starting at the upper right, multiply the two digits (7 x 3), and write the product (21) in the appropriate box in the grid. In writing the number, draw a diagonal line

in the box, and write one digit above the line and the other below it (2/1).

- Continue to multiply pairs of digits (7 x 6; then 7 x 5; and so on) and write the products in the boxes with diagonal lines (4/2; then 3/5; and so on). If a product has a single digit (9 for example) write it with a 0 before the digit (0/9).

- After all pairs of digits have been multiplied, add along the "diagonal," starting in the lower right corner and placing the answer at the bottom. "Carry" any tens digits to the next diagonal.

Again, challenge students to work in pairs to apply the al-Khwarizmi method to other multiplication problems. Ask students to explain why this method "works." (Suggest that they compare it with the method they use every day.)

Extension
Ask students to identify modern uses of Roman numerals. (Possible uses include diplomas, clock faces, and outlines.) Ask students why they think this system is still used.

This activity is an excellent opportunity for collaboration between social studies and math teachers. What better way to teach place value and demonstrate the use of zero!

Dale and Steve

THE COIN OF THE REALM: EXCHANGING CURRENCY

The barter system of trading goods was used at the early trade fairs, and few coins changed hands. But as these fairs attracted travelers from afar, money-changers were needed to figure out the value of the different currencies the travelers brought with them. In this activity, students explore the concept of currency exchange and create currency for use at their Medieval fair.

When You Can Use It

Q1: Who were the people of the Middle Ages?

Q3: What was daily life like then?

★Q5: How did people in the Middle Ages help shape our world today?

Objectives

■ **Math:** to compare/contrast currencies; to exchange currencies

■ **Social Studies:** to research the history of money

■ **English:** to participate in trade simulations

■ **Art:** to design and "print" currency

What You Might Assess

■ understanding of currency exchange

■ active participation in the simulation and/or role play

Materials and Resources

■ Examples of several modern currencies

■ Encyclopedias, *The Story of Money* by Betsy Maestro (Houghton Mifflin, 1993) and other resource books

HOW TO GO ABOUT IT

1. If possible, display some examples of modern currencies for students. Try to include some coins from various countries. Ask students how they would go about buying things in other countries—if they had only American coins with them. How might they obtain coins usable in the country they were in?

2. Invite students to do some research on the history of money. Share pictures of some old currencies with them. (These are available in most encyclopedias under the topic Money.) You might point out that when Marco Polo visited China in the 1200s, he was amazed to find people using paper money instead of coins. Mention that in Medieval Europe, most currency was in the form of coins, which were often made from silver and other heavy metals.

3. Encourage speculation about the limitations of currency in Medieval Europe. Why might it be inconvenient to carry around lots of silver and gold coins? Why might it be dangerous? Why might someone in one area not want to accept coins from another area in payment for goods or services? You might have students choose something equally inconvenient—perhaps different kinds of rocks—to carry around and use as a medium of exchange in a classroom simulation.

4. Discuss the role of the money-changer in Medieval society. Point out that at most fairs, the money-changer sat on a bench, or "banc," and exchanged coins for the customers. Ask which modern-day institution gets its name from the money-changer's bench. Then have students imagine that they are buyers or sellers at a Medieval fair, and supply them with "coins" (rocks or anything else students choose to use). Ask another group—the money-changers—to establish a rate of exchange for these "coins." Have students role play getting their money exchanged and then using it to "trade."

5. If students plan to have a Medieval fair, have them design and "print" currency that might be used to purchase goods and/or services.

Extension

Divide the class into groups, and assign each group a modern currency to research. Make sure that each group includes a dollar conversion rate in its report, and when all groups have presented their findings, assist the class in creating a modern currency conversion table on the board or on chart paper.

DIET: PREPARING A MEDIEVAL MENU

What did people of the Middle Ages eat? In this activity, students discover that Medieval meals varied greatly—depending on one's station in life. In fact, the peasantry enjoyed a much more healthful diet than did the nobility. And, except in times of famine, most people in Europe had an ample supply of food. If you plan to hold a Medieval banquet, this activity is a must!

When You Can Use It
★**Q1:** Who were the people of the Middle Ages?
★ **Q3:** What was daily life like then?

Objectives
■ **Social Studies:** to do research; to construct charts
■ **Science/Health:** to compare/contrast diets and their effects
■ **Home Ec:** to locate appropriate recipes

What You Might Assess
■ ability to locate information
■ inclusion of appropriate foods in proposed menus
■ ability to use a food-guide pyramid to evaluate diets

Materials and Resources
■ *A Medieval Feast* by Aliki (Crowell, 1983)—a picture book, also available as a sound filmstrip from SRA (Macmillan/McGraw-Hill)
■ *The Middle Ages* by Morris Bishop (Houghton Mifflin, 1987)
■ *Fabulous Feasts: Medieval Cookery and Ceremony* by Madeleine Pelner Cosman (Braziller, 1976)

HOW TO GO ABOUT IT

Beforehand
You may want to share *A Medieval Feast* with students as a warm-up for this activity. This picture book describes a fictitious Medieval feast. You may also want to read aloud or make available to students those sections of Morris Bishop's book, *The Middle Ages*, that deal with foods consumed by various groups (see the index).

1. Point out that what Medieval people ate varied greatly—depending on where they lived and what their station in life was. If you've shared the information from the Bishop book with students, you may want to have them make a chart similar to the one below. Have students fill in the specific foods.

What Medieval People Ate:			
Bourgeois	Monks	Nobles	Peasants
meat	fish	meat (lots)	pig
fish	eggs	fish	beans
cheese	cheese	fowl	cereals
white bread	dark bread	white bread	dark bread
eggs	eggs	eggs	turnips
pasta	beans	pastries (lots)	beans
pancakes	vegetables		leeks/onions
puddings			fruits

2. Discuss with students the concept of seasonal availability. Point out that preserving foods was an important consideration in the Middle Ages—since there was no means of refrigeration. Have students do some research to find out how foods were preserved. (Salt was used extensively, as were spices, which tended to hide the bad taste of foods on the verge of spoiling.) Also ask students to find out how foods were cooked. (Fowl and smaller animals were sometimes roasted on a spit, but most meat was boiled in order to tenderize it.)

3. Have students do more extensive research to find out about the foods they would have eaten—in their Medieval roles. Encourage students to plan a menu for a typical meal. Challenge students to try to find recipes for preparing one or more of the dishes.

HERBS: GROWING YOUR OWN

Medieval cooks used herbs and spices to flavor and preserve foods. During the Middle Ages, herbs were also valued for their medicinal qualities. The book Physica, written during the 12th century, includes herbal remedies for curing such things as coughs and ulcers and for treating wounds. In this activity, students explore the use of herbs in the Middle Ages—and today.

When You Can Use It
Q1: Who were the people of the Middle Ages?

★ **Q3:** What was daily life like then?

Q5: How did people in the Middle Ages help shape our world today?

Objectives
- **Social Studies:** to do research; to trace the origins of herbs
- **Science:** to investigate medicinal uses of herbs; to grow an herb garden

What You Might Assess
- the accuracy of students' research

Materials and Resources
- *The Middle Ages* by Morris Bishop (Houghton Mifflin, 1987)
- *Life in Medieval Times* by Marjorie Rowling (Putnam, 1979)
- *The Complete Book of Herbs & Spices* by Sarah Garland (Viking, 1979)
- *The Complete Book of Spices* by Jill Norman (Viking, 1990).
- Samples of fresh and dried herbs (basil, parsley, mint, etc.)
- Seeds, soil, planters, and other gardening implements

HOW TO GO ABOUT IT

1. Discuss with students what herbs are and how they are produced. Point out their various uses: in cooking, in making cosmetics, and as home remedies. You might mention that even medicines bought in a drug store go back to nature. (Aspirin was originally made from the bark of willow trees; penicillin from fungus; and digitalis from foxglove leaves.)

2. Point out that in the Middle Ages, herbs such as marigold and sage were used cosmetically; echinacea and golden seal, sage, and garlic were used medicinally; thyme, rosemary, parsley, and cinnamon were used in cooking. Have students do some research to find out how people in Medieval Europe obtained the herbs and spices they longed for. (Both of the books about herbs listed above include such information in their introductions.) Lead students to conclude that some were grown in manor gardens, while others were brought from afar by Medieval traders. Ask each student to choose two or three different herbs to "trace."

3. Invite students to share what they know about the use of herbs in cooking and in "healing."

You may want to mention these medicinal uses:

- Parsley—a source of Vitamin C, this herb has long been used as a breath freshener; it is now being studied for its potential in fighting cancer.

- Fennel—Native to the Mediterranean and Asia Minor, this herb serves as a muscle relaxant and to cure indigestion.

- Mint—Has long been used as an anesthetic for minor pains and to ease sore throats and stomach aches.

Ask students why they think herbs are making such a "comeback" today. Then invite students to investigate the herbs in use in their own households.

4. Invite students to plant a class herb garden. You will need seeds or seedlings, gardening supplies, and an appropriate space in the classroom. (Of course, an outdoor site will serve just as well, but this may not always be practical.)

FEASTS: "HOSTING" A MEDIEVAL BANQUET

In this activity, students learn how to host a Medieval feast. They discover that a seating plan was a most important consideration, and that certain rules of etiquette were followed. What students will probably enjoy most, however, is planning the menu for a Medieval banquet.

When You Can Use It

Q1: Who were the people of the Middle Ages?

Q2: How was Medieval society organized?

Q3: What was daily life like then?

★ **Q4:** What values and ideas were important in Medieval culture?

Objectives

- **Social Studies:** to research customs; to compare/contrast
- **Math:** to make scale drawings and diagrams
- **English:** to role play
- **Science/Home Ec:** to prepare a Medieval Menu

What You Might Assess

- accuracy of scale drawings and diagrams
- active participation in the role plays and/or simulations

Materials and Resources

- *A Medieval Feast* by Aliki (Crowell, 1983)—picture book
- *Fabulous Feasts: Medieval Cookery and Ceremony* by Madeleine Pelner Cosman (George Braziller, 1979)—advanced students
- Calculators; pencils and paper

HOW TO GO ABOUT IT

Beforehand

If you haven't already shared *A Medieval Feast* with students, this would be a wonderful time to do so. The author's note at the end of the book is an especially good warm-up for this activity.

1. Begin by asking students if they have ever attended a banquet or ceremonial dinner. What was the atmosphere like? What kinds of foods were served? Explain that during the Middle Ages holidays and other special occasions were usually marked by banquets (at least among the nobility).

2. Invite students who have taken on the roles of nobility to describe for classmates the kinds of foods eaten at a typical Medieval banquet. Have students work with partners or in small groups to prepare scale drawings of the floor plans and seating arrangements of the great halls where feasts took place.

3. Encourage your "noble" students to demonstrate for classmates some of the "etiquette" involved in feasting. For example:

- A trumpeter announces the start of the meal.
- Everyone washes hands—with honored guests using a washbowl and others a lavabo (basin) by the door.

- Everyone brings their own knives with them; spoons (but no forks) are provided. Fingers may be used for eating; the little finger is used to salt one's food. Fingers should not, however, be poked in eggs.

- Couples sitting next to each other share trenchers (wooden bowls).

- A blessing is given or "grace" is said. Then servants bring in the food.

- Hands are again washed at the end of the meal.

You may want to have a few students copy these rules of etiquette onto chart paper for display. Encourage them to do some research to find out about other rules.

We like to engage students in role plays during this activity. We invite students to pretend that they are at a Medieval feast during one lunch period. Students must use the rules of etiquette outlined above as they eat their lunches. We request that students pretend to be living in Medieval times and converse accordingly. No talking about TV or video games!

Dale

STUDENT PROJECT: FACTS AND FEELINGS

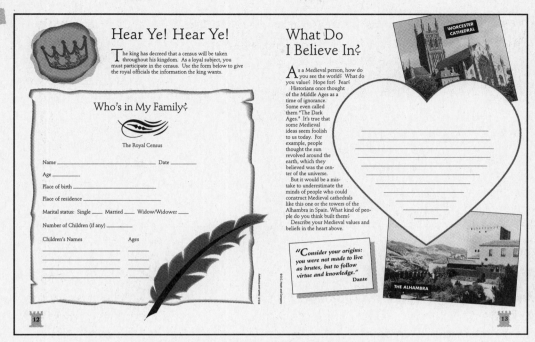

Student Project Book, pages 12 and 13

When You Can Use It

★ **Q4:** What values and ideas were important in Medieval culture?

Objectives

■ **Science Studies:** to do research

■ **English:** to synthesize research; to write a first-person essay

Materials and Resources

■ "Medieval Voices" in the Herald, pages 34-37

■ "Medieval Heroes" in the Herald, pages 42-43

■ For information about Medieval families: *Marriage and Family in the Middle Ages* by Frances and Joseph Gies

MANAGEMENT TIPS

✔ **PAGE 12** Tell students that our information about the size of families during the Middle Ages is sketchy. However, scholars agree that most families were probably small, including no more than three children. We know more about wealthy families than peasant ones, and there is evidence that wealthier families were often larger.

✔ **PAGE 13** Point out to students that the statement of belief on page 13 should be written in the first-person, using the pronoun "I". Ask students to be a specific as possible in describing the beliefs of their Medieval person. If students need more room, they can write on a separate piece of paper or on a computer.

✔ Remind students that not all Medieval Europeans were Christian. In Spain in particular, there were many Jews and Muslims. Students should consider the time and place where their Medieval person's story is set when writing their essay.

CODE OF BEHAVIOR: GRAPHING GOOD DEEDS

In this activity, students discover that human behavior in the Middle Ages was grounded in religious thought and in the knight's code of chivalry. After consciously observing good deeds for a few days, students become very aware of other people's behavior, including that of their teachers. So be very careful, if not downright chivalric.

When You Can Use It

Q1: Who were the people of the Middle Ages?

Q2: How was Medieval society organized?

★ **Q4:** What values and ideas were important in Medieval culture?

★ **Q5:** How did people in the Middle Ages help shape our world today?

Objectives

■ **Social Studies:** to do research

■ **Math:** to graph data

What You Might Assess

■ extent of contributions to small-group discussion

■ ability to record data on line or bar graphs

Materials and Resources

■ *Age of Chivalry* by Thomas Bulfinch (Airmont, 1965)

■ *The Age of Chivalry* by Abigail Frost (Marshall Cavendish, 1990)

■ *The End of Chivalry* (Marshall Cavendish, 1990)

■ Graph paper

HOW TO GO ABOUT IT

1. Point out to students that every culture has its own code of behavior. You might lead a discussion about our own society's written or unwritten codes. For example, American men are expected to wear jackets and ties for certain formal occasions. Point out that during the Middle Ages, the code of behavior was grounded in religious thought and in the knight's code of chivalry:

To be brave,

To maintain the right,

To redress the wrong,

To protect women,

To help those in trouble, and

To show mercy to the weak and defenseless.

2. Have students meet in small groups to discuss the code of chivalry. They might consider:

■ Does our own society subscribe to any of the same values? Which ones?

■ Is there any similarity between the knight's code and our school's code of behavior?

■ How has the role of women changed since the time of the Middle Ages? Why do you think Medieval women needed protecting?

3. Discuss with students why good deeds are often the product of a code of behavior. Suggest that students keep a record of any good deeds they observe being done for a period of two days. These deeds may include but are not limited to politeness, helpfulness, and selflessness. Have students make bar graphs to show the results of their observations.

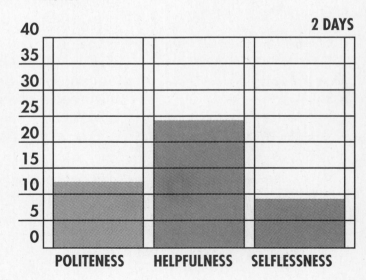

66 ACTIVITY BANK

THE MIDDLE AGES TEAM PLANNING GUIDE

HERALDRY: DESIGNING COATS OF ARMS

In this activity, students learn about heraldry and make their own coats of arms. It's a favorite with our students. Not only do they like personalizing their own coats of arms, but they also enjoy sharing their real ones. Students realize how many cultures are represented on their team, how last names have changed, and what mottoes mean. They discover that each part of a coat of arms has significance.

When You Can Use It

Q1: Who were the people of the Middle Ages?

Q3: What was daily life like then?

★ **Q4:** What values and ideas were important in Medieval culture?

Objectives

- **Social Studies:** to do research; torelate past to present
- **English:** to interpret symbols
- **Art:** to create designs incorporating symbols

What You Might Assess

- ability to follow the directions to create coats of arms
- articulation of reasons for students' choice of symbols

Materials and Resources

- Encyclopedias
- *Harold the Herald: A Book About Heraldry* by Dana Fradon (Dutton, 1990) and other books about heraldry
- Art supplies

HOW TO GO ABOUT IT

1. Share several examples of coats of arms with students. (Most encyclopedia articles on heraldry include pictures.) Point out that coats of arms were first used on the shields of Medieval knights. Later, other members of the nobility, and the clergy also acquired them. Ask students to identify the colors typically used on the coats of arms, and to describe some of the designs.

2. Have students design their own coats of arms. (Invite those students who are not members of the nobility or the clergy to temporarily step out of their Medieval roles for this activity.) Suggest that students follow the steps below.

- Using a piece of white construction paper, cut out the basic shield shape. (Students might fold the paper in half before cutting so that the shape is symmetrical.)

- Decide the first divisions for the shield. Choose from among the following:

Per Pale

Per Fesse

Quarterly

Per Blend

Per Blend Sinister

Per Chevron

Tersed in Pairle Reversed

Tersed in Fesse

- Decide on the colors to be used. (In Medieval times, the colors typically used were silver or white, black, blue, red, gold, green, and purple.) Color the parts of the shield.

- Using another piece of paper, design a charge. (A charge is a figure such as an animal, a ship, a turret, or a sword.)

- Cut out the charge and paste it onto the coat of arms.

- Add a cadency symbol. This shows the order of your birth. Choose from these symbols:

Order of Birth	Cadency Symbol	
1		(file or label)
2		(crescent)
3		(mullet)
4		(martlet)
5		(annulet)
6		(fleur-de-lis)
7		(rose)
8		(cross moline)
9		(octofoil)

- If you'd like, add a motto.

3. Encourage students to share their completed designs with classmates. Ask them to give reasons for their choice of colors and symbols.

4. Suggest that students transfer their designs onto large pieces of cardboard. They can use their coats of arms as decorations for their Medieval fair or banquet. Or, they can be displayed in the classroom.

Extension
Point out that today in the United States, anyone can create and use a coat of arms—called "arms of assumption." Students may enjoy creating such coats of arms for their own families. Encourage them to challenge classmates to decode the symbolism on their completed shields. Interested students may want to research and report on the origins of heraldry or on the practical role that it played in Medieval life. (They identified leaders in battle.)

> I brought in my own coat of arms to start off this activity. The helmet on my crest faces sideways—indicating that I am not descended from royalty. Also, atop my crest is a deer. That, along with the motto, shows how much my family likes nature.
>
> Dale

HEROES: RESPONDING TO LITERATURE

Students are often able to recognize heroic qualities in characters they read about in literature. In this activity, students read about Medieval heroes—both fictional and nonfictional. They also identify the heroic qualities of people living in contemporary times—and write tributes to those people. Through the activity, students become aware of the fact that everyday, ordinary people can also be heroes.

When You Can Use It

Q1: Who were the people of the Middle Ages?

★ **Q4:** What values and ideas were important in Medieval culture?

Objectives

- **Social Studies:** to identify heroes/heroic qualities
- **Literature:** to read stories set in Medieval times
- **English:** to compose poems of tribute
- **Art:** to design medals

What You Might Assess

- ability to identify characters and heroic qualities
- inclusion of vivid details and imagery in students' poems

Materials and Resources

- Books set in Medieval times, such as:

The Door in the Wall: A Story of Medieval London by Marguerite de Angeli (Doubleday, 1989)

Queen Eleanor: Independent Spirit of the Medieval World by Polly Schoyer Brooks (Lippincott, 1983)

The Whipping Boy by Sid Fleischman (Greenwillow, 1986)

See bibliography for other books

HOW TO GO ABOUT IT

1. Lead a discussion on what makes a person heroic. Students will probably suggest such qualities as bravery in the face of physical danger, courage in dealing with a personal loss, perseverance in overcoming a problem, and so on. Ask students to list some contemporary figures whom they think of as heroes.

2. Display books about Medieval heroes. You may want to give a quick book talk about one or more of the titles. Then have each student choose a book that he or she would like to read. Assign students to cooperative groups so that students who have read the same book can discuss it. In their discussion circles, students might consider:

- Who are the main characters of the book?

- What heroic qualities do these characters possess? How do they demonstrate those qualities?

- Do the characters have any weaknesses? If so, what are they? Does a character's weakness make him or her less of a hero? Why or why not?

3. During the Middle Ages, a person was sometimes rewarded for performing a heroic deed. These rewards might include a grant of money, land, or a medal. Ask each student to create a design for such a medal—that is, a reward for heroism. Point out that the design of the medal should in some way reflect its purpose. When medals are done, have students share their work.

Extension

Ask volunteers to write down the details of an heroic event they have seen, heard about, or imagined. Then ask them to write a poem about this event, utilizing as many details as possible. (You might remind them of the form of the epic poem.) Then have volunteers present their poems to classmates.

THE BEST POLICY: JOURNAL WRITING

In this activity, students explore the meanings of some phrases that originated in the Middle Ages. They then write in their journals about the topic of honesty. Since the activity centers on ethical issues, we don't require students to share their journal entries.

When You Can Use It
★ **Q4:** What values and ideas were important in Medieval culturet?

Objectives
■ **English:** to interpret idioms; to write journal entries; to explore word/phrase origins; to brainstorm lists

What You Might Assess
■ contributions to group discussion and/or brainstorming.
■ amount of time spent writing privately in personal journals.

Materials and Resources
■ Students' personal journals

HOW TO GO ABOUT IT

1. Point out to students that many common English words and phrases originated in Medieval times. The sports terms "first string" and "second string" once referred to the strings of an archer's bow. We still call the right side of a boat the "starboard" side because Anglo-Saxon boats had a "steering board" on the right side. Because of that, only the ship's left side could be pulled alongside a wharf at port, making that the "port" side. When a person acts in an especially generous way, we still say they are "chivalrous."

2. Tell students that in Medieval markets, a dishonest trader would sell a pig to a customer and then substitute a cat in its place. How could he get away with this? The trader would hand the customer his purchase in a bag, which was then called a poke. Eventually, though, word of such dishonest deals would spread, and when future customers bought "a pig in a poke," they would open the poke on the spot and "let the cat out of the bag." Remind students that later in the Middle Ages, laws were passed to prevent such commercial deceits.

3. Ask students to respond to these questions in their journals:

■ What does the phrase "pig in a poke" mean today? Have you ever felt deceived by a purchase you made? Tell about it.

■ Think of a time when you "let the cat out of the bag." Describe the experience and how you felt about it.

4. Present students with this expression: "Honesty is the best policy."

Consider asking students a question such as: "Is it ever appropriate to lie or to steal?" Stress that you would like frank answers, and be prepared for a stimulating discussion!

5. Ask students to prepare another entry for their personal journals. This one should detail a situation in which honesty was the best policy for the student. Be sure to point out that students need not share their journal entries with anyone, unless they choose to do so.

6. Have students work in small groups to brainstorm and list occasions in the world today in which honesty is important. Encourage them to give reasons for their thinking.

Extension
Encourage students to find other words and expressions that have their origins in the Middle Ages. To get them started, you might suggest "below the salt" and "not worth his/her salt."

STUDENT PROJECT: WHERE DO I DWELL?

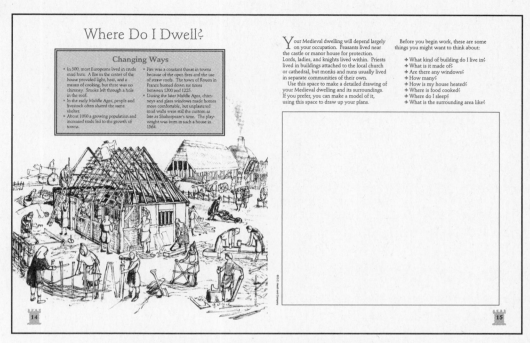

Student Project Book, pages 14 and 15

When You Can Use It

Q1: Who were the people of the Middle Ages?

★ **Q3:** What was daily life like then?

Objectives

■ **Science Studies:** to do research

Materials and Resources

■ For information about Medieval houses: *Life in a Medieval Village* by Frances and Joseph Gies

■ For models: sticks, straw, mud (or clay), modeling clay

MANAGEMENT TIPS

✔ The Medieval house shown under construction on page 14 is from a village in England. The kinds of construction used for houses varied throughout Europe, depending on the materials available. People in Northern Europe often used wood for their homes, because tall trees were abundant there. Houses in Spain, Italy, and southern France were often built of stone or brick.

✔ Encourage students to make scale models of their Medieval dwellings, using the space on page 15 to draw plans. Since many peasant huts were made of sticks, straw, and mud, authentic materials will be easy to find. Model castles can be constructed from modeling clay.

✔ The British still use thatching Medieval techniques. You might get a book from the library that shows thatchers at work.

TOWNS : CREATING SCALE MODELS

This is a hands-on project that involves students in researching, planning, and constructing a model of a typical Medieval town. Students can work together to create a single model, or several groups of students can create their own models. The project is time-consuming, but students become so involved and learn so much as a result that we think it's well worth the time spent.

When You Can Use It
Q1: Who were the people of the Middle Ages?
★ **Q3:** What was daily life like?

Objectives
■ **Social Studies:** to do research; to construct a replica of a Medieval town
■ **Math:** to apply scale measurement

What You Might Assess
■ ability to work effectively in cooperative groups
■ extent of each student's contribution in constructing model(s)

Materials and Resources
■ *Walter Dragun's Town* by Sheila Sancha (HarperCollins, 1989)
■ *Living in Castle Times* and *The Time Traveller Book of Knights & Castles* (Usborne, 1982, 1976)
■ Art supplies (including cardboard boxes of various sizes)

HOW TO GO ABOUT IT

Note: You may want to use this activity in conjunction with the one that follows on castles.

Beforehand
Sharing *Walter Dragun's Town* with students is a wonderful warm-up for this activity. Students will learn much from the aerial views and schematic drawings.

1. Suggest that students find as many pictures of Medieval towns as they can. Have them look especially for pictures that show how the towns were laid out. Encourage them to look for common features, such as the location of the church, the guildhall, the castle, and the shops and market stalls. Have them note the town walls, with gates that could be locked for the town's protection.

2. Tell students that in this activity, they will work in small groups to construct a model of a typical Medieval town. Several groups could contribute to a single model by dividing up the various tasks: planning the layout, making houses, constructing the castle or manor house, building the walls, etc. These tasks could be divided up according to students' Medieval roles (with members of the clergy responsible for the church; peasants, for the gardens and small huts, and so forth).

3. As students are planning their model(s), encourage them to collect materials they will use for building. They will need such things as cardboard boxes of varying sizes that can transformed into buildings; sponges that can be dipped in green paint and used for trees and bushes, etc. Encourage students to be creative and to put their scavenging skills to work here!

4. Provide a tabletop—and ample time—for actual construction of the town model(s). When they have finished, students may enjoy giving other classes a "guided tour" of their town(s).

Extension
Ask students to compare and contrast the typical Medieval town with today's shopping malls.

CASTLE: DESIGNING YOUR OWN

Students construct models of castles in this activity, which we often combine with the previous one. That way, one group of students, often our "clerics," can be planning and executing the castle while others are working on other features of the town. If you prefer to keep the two activities separate, you might have students make scale drawings for this activity.

When You Can Use It

Q1: Who were the people of the Middle Ages?

★ **Q3:** What was daily life like then?

Objectives

■ **Social Studies:** to do research about Medieval architecture

■ **Math:** to create a model and/or a scale drawing

What You Might Assess

■ understanding the function of each part of a castle

■ ability to work cooperatively to construct models and/or make scale drawings

Materials and Resources

■ *Castle* by David Macaulay (Houghton Mifflin, 1977)

■ *Castles* by Beth Smith (Franklin Watts, 1988)

■ *A Medieval Castle: Inside Story* by Fiona MacDonald (Peter Bedrick Books, 1990)

■ Art supplies

■ Math texts (lessons on ratio, proportion, scale drawing)

HOW TO GO ABOUT IT

1. Discuss the function of castles in Medieval life. Point out that people lived near the castle for protection, since raids by bandits and invaders were frequent.

2. Introduce students to the various parts of a typical castle. You may want to display a schematic drawing from one of the books listed above.

■ Outer Bailey: The first courtyard .

■ Inner Bailey: The inner courtyard, protected by two walls.

■ Curtain: This surrounded the inner courtyard; often ten or more feet thick.

■ Keep: This strong and heavily fortified area housed the owner and his family; designed to be the last line of defense.

■ Drawbridge: A bridge that could be raised or lowered, usually over a moat.

■ Parapets: Low walls around the top of a tower or castle wall.

■ Machicolations: Holes in the parapets used for dropping such things as boiling oil and stones on unwelcome "guests."

■ Arrow-loops: Narrow openings in the towers, for firing arrows.

■ Barbican: The forward gate, located before the main gate.

■ Postern Gate: A back gate used as a means of escape.

■ Portcullis: Main gate, made from heavy wood and reinforced with iron grating.

■ Murder Holes: Holes in the ceiling behind the front gate; used for dropping stones on attackers who got through the gate.

3. Tell students that they will now use their research to create a model or a scale drawing of a typical castle. (If students make scale drawings, they should label all the parts. You may want to review ratio, proportion, and the concept of scale before students get underway.)

On the next page is a drawing I did that you may want to duplicate for students' use.

Dale

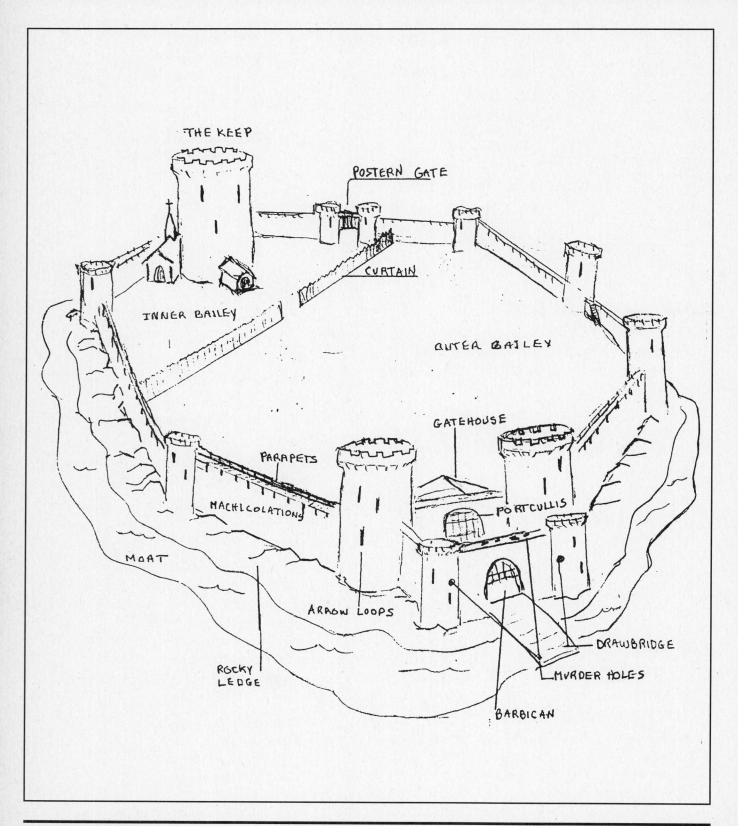

STUDENT PROJECT: AN ORDINARY DAY

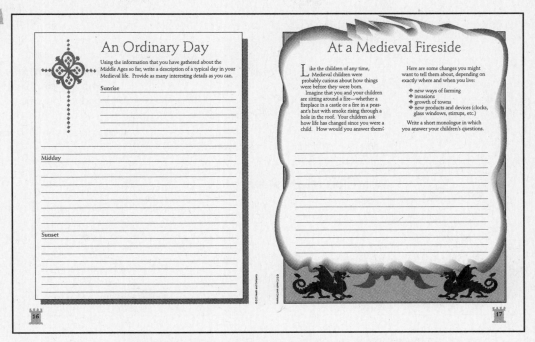

Student Project Book, pages 16 and 17

When You Can Use It

Q1: Who were the people of the Middle Ages?

★ **Q3:** What was daily life like then?

★ **Q5:** How did people in the Middle Ages help shape our world today?

Objectives

■ **Science Studies:** to do research; to analyze cause and effect

■ **English:** to write journal entries; to write monologues

MANAGEMENT TIPS

✔ **PAGE 16** Help students do some prewriting by listing all the daily activities they think their Medieval people might engage in. Then they can go through the list, indicating whether the activity would probably be done in the morning, afternoon, or the evening. They can use this list to prepare a journal entry on page 16.

✔ **PAGE 17** In writing monologues about the changes their Medieval people have seen, students can focus on one or more of the topics listed at the top of page 17. They also might focus on other events, such as the introduction of Arabic numbers or the Crusades. Ask students to explain specifically how these changes have affected their Medieval people personally.

✔ Remind students that the monologue should be written in the first person, using the pronoun "I."

LISTENING TO MEDIEVAL MUSIC

The music of the Middle Ages, sometimes called "early music," has become very popular among classical music fans in recent years, and most large record stores have a good selection of it. If you live near a metropolitan center or a university, you may even be able to take your class to a Medieval concert. Because it uses easily understood structures, much Medieval music is accessible and appealing.

When You Can Use It

★ **Q4:** What values and ideas were important in Medieval culture?

★ **Q5:** How did people in the Middle Ages help shape our world today?

Objectives

■ **English:** to compare and contrast; to write a music review

■ **Music:** to identify the basic features of a musical work

What You Might Assess

■ ability to compare and contrast

■ expository writing

Materials and Resources

■ These are some of the best recordings of Medieval music. All are available on both CDs and cassettes.

Benedictine Monks of Santo Domingo de Silos—This recording topped the pop record charts in early 1994. EMI 55138.

Music of the Crusades (13th-century French music, including music by Richard the Lionhearted)—Early Music Consort of London, Decca CD 430 264-2, cassette 430 264-4.

"Summer is icumen in" (Medieval English songs)—Hilliard Ensemble, Harmonia Mundi CD HMC 901154.

These records can be ordered from Serenade Record Shop, Washington DC (tele 202-783-0372; fax 202-638-6648).

HOW TO GO ABOUT IT

Beforehand

Listen to several recordings of Medieval music and find two selections that have strong rhythms or striking melodies that will appeal to students. Choose two that have contrasting features. For example, pick two that have markedly different tempos. Most recordings contain the lyrics, and you may want to provide copies to the class.

1. Ask students to speculate about how the music of the Middle Ages might have sounded. What instruments might have been used? Do students think that Medieval music had lyrics, like today's pop music, or was it purely instrumental?

2. After the discussion, play one of the selections for the class. Then use these questions to lead a discussion about the music.

■ Was the music what students expected? How was it different?

■ What kinds of rhythm did the music use? Was the melody interesting?

■ What patterns can students find in the music? Were certain lyrics or certain parts of the melody repeated?

3. Now play the second selection and help students compare the two pieces.

■ Were the rhythms of this piece different from those of the first? How? How was its melody different?

■ How were the patterns of this piece different?

■ Which one is more appealing? Why?

4. Ask students to compare and contrast Medieval music with modern music.

5. Allow students to borrow the recordings or listen to them on equipment in the school library. Have them write a brief music review of a single selection, using the discussion questions above as guidelines.

STUDENT PROJECT: My Medieval Story

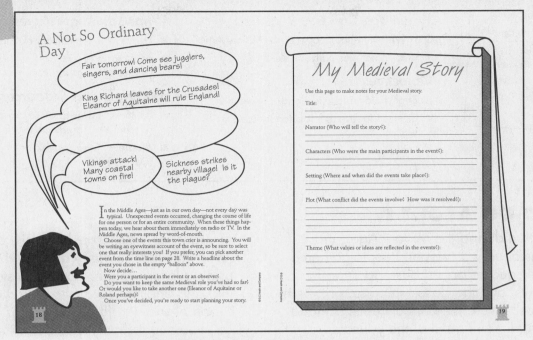

Student Project Book, pages 18 and 19

When You Can Use It

Q1: Who were the people of the Middle Ages?

★ **Q2:** How was Medieval society organized?

★ **Q3:** What was daily life like then?

Objectives

- **Social Studies:** to do research
- **English:** to synthesize information; to make notes for a narrative

Materials and Resources

- "A Medieval Time Line" in The Herald, pages 28-29
- "Medieval Voices" in The Herald, pages 34-37
- "Medieval Heroes" in The Herald, pages 42-43
- A biography of a Medieval person (see Bibliography)

MANAGEMENT TIPS

✔ **PAGE 18** Students are choosing an event from the Middle Ages that they will use as the subject of a presentation. If the stories will be presented in written form, students can choose and plan their stories individually. If the stories will take the form of graphic or dramatic presentations (see page 83), it will probably be most effective for students to work in groups. You may want to create those groups before doing pages 18 through 21 so that each group can choose its event together.

✔ **PAGE 19** This activity gives students a chance to plan their Medieval stories, either individually or in groups. If students are planning dramatic presentations, you might do a separate planning session with each group, listing the six elements of story planning (see Student Book page) on the blackboard. When you have planned the story together, students can record the elements of the story here.

WRITING, MEDIEVAL STYLE

In this activity, students use Medieval tools to write letters and/or invitations. You may want to display examples of calligraphy for students' reference as they work.

When You Can Use It
Q1: Who were the people of the Middle Ages?
★ **Q3:** What was daily life like then?

Objectives
■ **English:** to write letters and/or invitations
■ **Science:** to research substances used in writing

What You Might Assess
■ creativity in the content of students' letters
■ correctness of each student's grammar, usage, and mechanics

Materials and Resources
■ Feathers, knives or other sharpening tools, parchment, ingredients for "ink"
■ *Medieval Calligraphy* by Marc Drogin (Dover, 1989)

HOW TO GO ABOUT IT

1. Explain that during the Middle Ages, most communication was verbal. People gathered in village squares or alehouses to hear the latest news, and the closest thing to a modern "news flash" were the announcements made by a herald. Point out that the educated nobles and the clergy did use written communication, however.

2. Tell students they will now write a letter using Medieval writing tools. Distribute feathers and help students sharpen them to make quill pens. Remind students that ink, like most products during the Middle Ages, had to be produced from materials on hand. Suggest that students do some research to find out what Medieval people used for ink. (Some Medieval inks were made from berries.)

3. If possible set up the materials for "ink-making" in one corner of the classroom, and have students make a small supply. They can make berry-based ink by crushing berries (blueberries, blackberries, strawberries, elderberries, or cherries) to make one cup of juice. This can be easily done in a strainer, using a large wooden spoon. To stabilize the ink, add one teaspoon of salt and one teaspoon of vinegar. (If ink-making is impractical, you might simply distribute small pots of commercial ink at this point.)

4. Have students write letters using these Medieval tools. They may write to friends or family members, or they may write to imaginary companions from the Middle Ages. If students choose the latter, suggest that they write their missives on scrolls (unlined paper that can be rolled up and tied with a piece of ribbon).

EXTENSION
The discussion of natural substances used for ink might lead to a similar discussion concerning dyes. Also, these discussions often kindle students' interest in calligraphy, and you might encourage them to make invitations for their Medieval fair using this form of writing.

THE VIKINGS ARE COMING! RECREATING AN EVENT

Students explore the influence of the Vikings on the Medieval world in this activity, which involves using map skills and critical thinking. They work in small groups to plan how they might defend themselves during a Viking raid. They also write poetry about the Vikings or about their imagined experiences during a Viking raid.

When You Can Use It

Q1: Who were the people of the Middle Ages?

★ **Q3:** What was daily life like?

Objectives

- **Social Studies:** to trace routes on a map; to propose solutions to problems
- **English:** to compose poems
- **Literature:** to read and report on Viking mythology and/or poetry

What You Might Assess

- ability to use research to trace routes on a map
- understanding of the defense mechanisms of Medieval towns
- creativity reflected in students' poems

Materials and Resources

- *Life in the Time of Harald Hardrada and the Vikings* by Peter Speed (Richard Hook, 1993)
- *Over Nine Hundred Years Ago: With the Vikings* and *The Vikings* by Hazel M. Martell (Macmillan, 1993)
- *The Vikings* by Pamela Odijk (Silver Burdett, 1990)

HOW TO GO ABOUT IT

1. Have students locate Scandinavia, the home of the Vikings, on a map. Point out that while many Norsemen ("men of the north") were warlike raiders, others were traders and settlers. All, however, were fearless seafarers. Ask students to do some research to find out the extent of Viking influence on the world of the Middle Ages. You may want to divide the class up into three groups, with different groups responsible for researching Danish, Norwegian, and Swedish Vikings. Have students trace the major routes followed by these seafarers on a world map.

2. Ask students to imagine that they are the occupants of a small village which is about to be attacked by a Viking party. As the warning bells toll and the villagers rush for the safety of the castle, how will the various people prepare for the attack? Have students work in small groups to brainstorm ideas and to propose plans for their self-defense. Some research may be required, but students will need to use their imaginations, too.

3. Once students have shared their proposals, ask why the Vikings were feared by so many other peoples of the Middle Ages. Then remind the class that the Vikings made considerable contributions to European culture. Ask them to research what these contributions were and then to summarize their findings under two headings: Skills and Cultural Contributions. Under Skills, students might list such things as shipbuilding (using keels), navigation, and warfare; under Cultural Contributions, they might list poetry, metalworking and woodcarving, and mythology. (Students may be interested to know that several of our names for days of the week derive from Norse mythology.)

4. Invite students to compose poems about the Vikings or about their imagined experiences during a Viking raid.

Extension

Encourage interested students to research and report on Viking mythology and/or the literature (especially the sagas).

THE CRUSADES: RESEARCHING AND REPORTING

Historians sometimes speak of the Crusades as a single event, but the term refers to a series of holy wars between European Christians and Middle Eastern Muslims that stretched over a period of 174 years. In this activity, students learn about the key people and events of the Crusades.

When You Can Use It

Q1: Who were the people of the Middle Ages?

★ **Q2:** What values and ideas were important in Medieval culture?

★ **Q3:** How did people in the Middle Ages help shape our world today?

Objectives

■ **Social Studies:** to do research; to report; to read and make maps

What You Might Assess

■ students' ability to locate and use a variety of resource materials including maps; creativity of students' methods of presentation; accuracy of information.

Materials and Resources

■ A Medieval Time Line, The Herald, pages 28-29

■ Encylopedias and other reference books

HOW TO GO ABOUT IT

Background

"Jerusalem is a land fruitful above all others, a paradise of delights. That royal city, situated at the center of the earth, implores you to come to her aid. Undertake this journey eagerly for the remission of your sins, and be assured of the reward of imperishable glory in the Kingdom of Heaven."

With these words, Pope Urban II in 1095 urged the people of Europe to launch a holy war against the Turks. The Muslim Turks had seized control of Palestine and were denying Christians access to Jerusalem, a city considered holy by Jews, Christians, and Muslims. The Pope's idea caught the imagination of people throughout western Europe, and the next year a huge army, headed by 50,000 knights, set off for the Middle East.

1. Pope Urban's words make the Crusades sound like a noble quest, and many Christians saw it that way. But the Pope had other concerns, too. Europe had been racked by war, and the Pope hoped a common enemy might unite people. Have students do research to find out about the mixed motives of the following groups involved in the Crusades: knights, merchants, the clergy.

2. Just reaching Palestine took the Crusaders three years. Have students research the routes they took and trace them on a map. Students can create a chart detailing some of the problems the army confronted along the way: geographical obstacles, like the Alps; the perils of travel by boat; the need to buy or seize food and other supplies enroute.

3. Most of the Crusaders never reached Jerusalem. They gave up and turned back or died in fighting or of disease. Finally in June of 1099 the remaining force of about 12,000 attacked Jerusalem. Have students write an eye-witness account of the siege of Jerusalem from the viewpoint of one of the following participants:

■ a Christian knight

■ a Muslim soldier defending the city

■ a Jewish scholar living in the city

4. There were three other major Crusades and several smaller ones. Have students research one of the following people who took part in them: Eleanor of Aquitaine, King Richard the Lion Hearted, Pope Innocent III.

THE BLACK DEATH: ANALYZING ITS IMPACT

In the 1300s, the Black Death swept over Europe, killing at least a third of the population of France, England, and Italy. Because of the close proximity in which their people lived, manors and monasteries were hardest hit. In this activity, students explore the effects of the Black Death on Medieval society.

When You Can Use It

Q1: Who were the people of the Middle Ages?

★ **Q3:** What was daily life like then?

Objectives

- **Social Studies:** to do research; to interpret maps and charts; to compare/contrast; to identify cause/effect relationships; to relate past to present
- **English:** to brainstorm solutions to problem situations; to identify cause/effect relationships; to write explanatory paragraphs

What You Might Assess

- ability to interpret maps and charts
- understanding of cause and effect
- contributions to brainstorming sessions
- inclusion of supporting details in explanatory paragraphs

Materials and Resources

- The Herald, pages 40-41
- *The Black Death* by Timothy Biel (Lucent Books, 1989)

HOW TO GO ABOUT IT

1. Have students read "The Black Death" on pages 40-41 of The Herald. Have students locate China on a world map. (You might point out that the bubonic plague did not originate in China. The first recorded cases of plague occurred in ancient Greece in the fifth century BC.) Invite speculation about how the plague was carried from China to Italy. Then have students use the map on page 41 to trace the spread of the plague in Europe. Relate the information imparted by the map to that contained in the chart.

2. Tell students that although no one knows exactly how many people died from the plague, it's estimated that Medieval Europe lost at least a third of its total population— and probably more. Ask students to consider the impact of such a loss on Medieval society. On many manors, there were not enough serfs to do the required work. Those serfs who did survive were in a position to make some demands for themselves, and many fled their manors in hope of improving their lives. How did the plague such things as farming, communication, trade, church, individual families? Ask students to write paragraphs in which they explain one or more of the effects of the plague on Medieval society.

3. Divide the class into small groups, and then have students brainstorm the following situations:

- As a serf, untouched by the plague, you find that your personal value to the lord has increased. How do you handle the situation?

- As a noble, faced with fewer workers to maintain your lifestyle, you find yourself forced to listen to new demands. What are these demands and how will you handle them?

4. The most recent large outbreak of plague began in 1894. It killed 10 million people in India alone. Ask students whether there are any modern-day plagues, and what effect they have on our society. Then join the students in comparing such modern-day plagues as AIDS to the Black Death. How are the two epidemics similar? How are they different? How has modern medicine affected our ability to cope with such a disaster?

REDISCOVERING MEDIEVAL WOMEN

In the last ten years, there has been an explosion of scholarship on women's role in the Middle Ages. What's surprising is that Medieval women were never systemically studied before, given the fact that many wealthy women were literate and left writings that provide a wealth of detail about their lives.

When You Can Use It

Q1: Who were the people of the Middle Ages?

Q3: What was daily life like then?

Q4: What values and ideas were important in Medieval culture?

★ **Q5:** How did people in the Middle Ages help shape our world today?

Objectives

- **Social Studies:** to understand gender discrimination; to relate past to present
- **English:** to write a biographical sketch

What You Might Assess

- accuracy and appropriateness of information
- ability to synthesize information
- ability to relate past to present

Materials and Resources

- These works of fiction and non-fiction feature female protagonists from the Middle Ages:

    Queen Eleanor: Independent Spirit of the Medieval World by Polly Schoyer Brooks (Lippincott, 1983)

    Lost Magic by Berthe Amoss (Little, Brown, 1993)

    See Bibliography for other books.

HOW TO GO ABOUT IT

1. Begin this activity by helping students to understand how we learn about past events. Ask students to name the event that Americans celebrate on the Fourth of July (the anniversary of the Declaration of Independence in 1776). Now ask students how they know about the Declaration. Have they heard about it from eyewitnesses? Have they read eyewitness accounts about it?

2. The answer to the first question is, of course, no; the answer to the second is probably no, too. Students probably don't have any knowledge of the Declaration from what are called primary sources; they know about it from secondary sources: a social studies book, a work of historical fiction like *Johnny Tremain*, or maybe a parent or friend who explained the holiday to them without having firsthand experience of the Declaration themselves.

3. Explain that most historical knowledge is transmitted in this way. We could learn about the Declaration from letters, diaries, and newspapers of the time, but, for the most part, only scholars do that. Most of us depend on a secondary source to learn about events from the past.

4. Point out that until recently most history was written by men. Male historians tended to focus primarily on the actions of other men. This was especially true when they wrote about a period like the Middle Ages, when few women were allowed to take part in public affairs, except as nuns or merchants.

5. Explain that today there are more female scholars than in the past, and that they are reexamining the role of women throughout history. In studying the Middle Ages, their research is aided by the fact that many wealthy Medieval women could read and write and have left detailed records of their lives. Some of the things we are learning are surprising. For example, the French writer Christine de Pisan tells us that women often hunted alongside men in Medieval hunting parties.

6. Assign students one of the books listed above to read (or another book set in the Middle Ages that has a female protagonist). Then have students write a brief biographical sketch about the person, comparing and contrasting her with a well-known American woman today.

STUDENT PROJECT: PLANNING A PRESENTATION

Telling the Story

Present your eyewitness account of the event you have chosen using any of the forms listed below. The items shown under the various types of dramatic presentations will tell you some of the resources you can use for that storytelling method.

WRITING
+ A short story
+ A journalistic account
+ A play
+ A poem or a song

GRAPHICS
+ A storyboard
+ A mural
+ A diorama

A DRAMATIC PRESENTATION
+ A play
  Script
  Actors
  Musicians
  Props
  Sets
  Costumes

+ A puppet show
  Script
  Puppets
  Actors/puppeteers
  Musicians
  Scenery
  Sound effects

+ A radio program
  Script
  Actors
  Sound effects
  Musicians
  Audio recorder and tape

+ A video
  Script
  Actors
  Musicians
  Props
  Sets
  Costumes

20

Planning Your Presentation

Here is a form you can use to plan the presentation of your Medieval story, whether you are working with a group or on your own. If you are working with a group, meet with the other group members and decide what jobs need to be done and who will do them. If you are working alone, use the "Who will do them" column to list others who might help you with details, so you will finish on time. In deciding when each task should be finished, make sure that you allow enough time.

Stages	Specific tasks to be done	Who will do them	Date of completion
Organization 1. finish research 2. outline or plan			
Construction draft or assemble			
Presentation Preparation 1. practice 2. peer review			

21

Student Project Book, pages 20 and 21

When You Can Use It

★ **Q1:** Who were the people of the Middle Ages?

Q2: How was Medieval society organized?

★ **Q3:** What was daily life like then?

Objectives

■ **Social Studies:** to do research; to understand cause and effect

■ **English:** to plan and organize a presentation; to write a narrative

Materials and Resources

■ For students planning a video presentation: *Learn To Make Videos in a Weekend* by Roland Lewis (Knopf, 1993) is an excellent and straightforward guide to using a camcorder.

■ Most encyclopedias have useful information about producing a play, radio program, or puppet show.

MANAGEMENT TIPS

✔ **PAGE 20** Guide students in choosing how they will tell their Medieval story. Consider how much time you have for this part of the unit, and help students plan a presentation they can realistically expect to complete in the allotted time.

✔ **PAGE 21** Students may need help in listing the specific tasks their presentation requires. If students are working in groups, you may want to do a separate planning session with each group. Students can record task assignments here.

This is the time to consider who in your school or community might be interested in providing support for the unit (see "Team Meeting," page 29). A teacher or parent might be a skilled puppeteer, camcorder operator, or musician. That person's participation can make the student presentation easier and more fun. Don't be reluctant to ask—most people will be flattered to be asked and glad to help.

THE PLAY'S THE THING! DRAMATIZATIONS

Many students love the chance to act. Don't think this requires a lot of fancy scenery and costumes. Kids can have a lot of fun—and also learn a lot—by doing Readers Theatre, where the parts are spoken but not "acted out." You can make this even more fun by recording it and adding music and sound effects to create a radio play!

When You Can Use It

Q1: Who were the people of the Middle Ages?

Q3: What was daily life like then?

Q4: What values and ideas were important in Medieval culture?

★ **Q5:** How did people in the Middle Ages help shape our world today?

Objectives

■ **Literature/English:** to read and discuss Medieval tales; to present dramatic interpretations of these tales

What You Might Assess

■ students' understanding of plot and characterization, as reflected in their dramatic presentations

■ quality of oral interpretation, including expression and audibility

Materials and Resources

■ The Herald, pages 34-37

■ Medieval tales, such as:

Canterbury Tales by Barbara Cohen (Morrow, 1988)

Robin Hood by Paul Creswick (Macmillan, 1984)

The Kitchen Knight: A Tale of King Arthur by Margaret Hodges (Holiday House, 1990)

HOW TO GO ABOUT IT

1. Point out to students that many masterworks of literature were written during the Middle Ages. You might mention the epics *Beowulf*, *Poem of the Cid*, *Song of Roland*, and *Nibelungenlied*; the romances about King Arthur; the short stories of Boccaccio and Chaucer; and of course Dante's *Divine Comedy*.

2. Encourage students to read "Medieval Voices" on pages 34-37 of The Herald. You might ask students to present a dramatic interpretation of one or more of these pieces.

3. Suggest that students work in cooperative groups to read and present a dramatization of one of the books suggested above (or others of your own choosing). Discuss the importance of being thoroughly familiar with such things as plot and characterization before attempting a dramatic re-enactment. Have students read the books they've selected and discuss them with others in their groups. Then have them choose a part to present dramatically.

4. Review with students the options for dramatic presentations, such as Readers Theatre, choral reading, dialogue improvisation, and performing from a prepared script. Have each group choose its own method. Allow time for students to prepare and rehearse their presentations.

Although students will want to "try out" their presentations on classmates, you may want to suggest that they give their "final" performances as part of the culminating experience for the unit. We've found that kids really like to "ham things up" once they have an audience other than their peers.

Moya

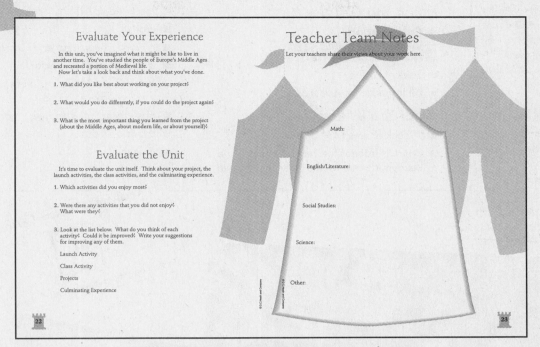

Evaluate Your Experience

In this unit, you've imagined what it might be like to live in another time. You've studied the people of Europe's Middle Ages and recreated a portion of Medieval life.
Now let's take a look back and think about what you've done.

1. What did you like best about working on your project?

2. What would you do differently, if you could do the project again?

3. What is the most important thing you learned from the project (about the Middle Ages, about modern life, or about yourself)?

Evaluate the Unit

It's time to evaluate the unit itself. Think about your project, the launch activities, the class activities, and the culminating experience.

1. Which activities did you enjoy most?

2. Were there any activities that you did not enjoy? What were they?

3. Look at the list below. What do you think of each activity? Could it be improved? Write your suggestions for improving any of them.

Launch Activity

Class Activity

Projects

Culminating Experience

Teacher Team Notes

Let your teachers share their views about your work here.

Math:

English/Literature:

Social Studies:

Science:

Other:

Student Project Book, pages 22 and 23

MANAGEMENT TIPS

✔ **PAGE 22** Suggest that students look back over their Student Project Books before answering the questions here. In particular, they should review the Guiding Questions on pages 6 and 7. Encourage students to evaluate the unit privately and honestly. After students have written their responses, a class discussion can bring out new points that didn't occur to students individually. Student feedback will help you and the team adapt the unit for future use.

✔ EVALUATION TIPS

PAGE 23 This page is designed to enable each team member provide written feedback to students. As you do so, feedback, consider these suggestions:

■ Note specifics—both positive and negative.

■ Tell students how they can improve in the future.

■ Focus on how students worked, as well as what they produced. For example, you might comment on the amount of effort and resourcefulness put into research or comment on students' ability to work with others.

A MEDIEVAL FAIR: SIMULATION

The headline in the Sarasota Independent read: "Medieval Fair takes students back to days of old." It was the day after our 1987 fair, and we all breathed a sigh of relief. Our first fair was a bit scary in that we weren't sure how donations of food and drink might go— among other things. But it all worked out— and our fair got a rave review.

When You Can Use It
★ Culmination

What Leads Up To It
- Student Project
- All Instructional Activities

What You'll Need
- a block of time (2 to 3 hours)
- grounds (rooms) for the booths that have been made and for the activities planned
- food and drink
- crafts
- a work schedule for each activity of Fair Day
- a time posted for special features
- props: extra Medieval "money," hole punches, gloves, signs
- trash receptacles, markers, game prizes
- tables and chairs
- costumes

Medieval Fair takes students back to days of old

JOANNE MAMENTA

Garbed in a long blue dress and a wreath of blue flowers topping her head, April Ford took a break in selling "dragon eyes" in order to eat her lunch.

Ford, a student at Sarasota Middle School, was one of 130 six-graders participating in a medieval fair at the school on Friday. Her dragon eyes are commonly known as popcorn balls.

"They just got finished studying the middle ages, learning about crusaders, trade fairs, feudalism. This is a culmination of the activities," said sixth-grade teacher Dale Crooke, who was dressed like an elf.

Crooke and three colleagues concocted the event for their "Spinnaker's team," the name given to the group of 130 students taught by the four teachers. There are two other six-grade teams at the school.

Typically, the students attend the annual medieval fair held at the Ringling Museum of Art.

The teachers hope this year the students will have a better appreciation of living in the middle ages.

"They've had to do research about knights and the medieval era and hopefully they'll take something with them when they go to the fair this year," Moya Hanaway, another sixth-grade teacher added.

Speaking to a number of the medieval lords, ladies, peasants, princesses, knights, jesters and jousters, it was apparent they knew something about the middle ages.

"We learned about manorialism, which was a way of life back then. It's when the lord owned land and he lives in a manor house and he has peasants, known as serfs, working for him.

"The serfs live in a village away from the manor," said David O'Brien, a 20th century Robin Hood dressed in a green polyester robe and a brown felt cap.

"They like to trade a lot and be in trade fairs. They meet people from other cultures who dress differently and lived differently," said Many Elson, a 12-year-old princess dressed in a mini-skirt and flowered head-piece.

In the medieval village on the north side of the school were a number of cardboard framed booths where peasants traded and sold goods.

While some students stood in line to buy "dragon's blood" at King Arthur's Pub, other students participated in a human checkers game.

Nathan Lawrence, dressed in a white shirt and black knickers and suspenders, got ready to participate in a jousting match.

His horse and shield were made of cardboard while a dust mop served as his lance.

Both Derek Conley and Patrick Harris said they would have enjoyed living in the middle ages. While the rest of their classmates were manning trade booths, Conley and Harris practiced sword fighting on the other side of the building.

Reprinted from the *Sarosota Independent*, Feb.21/22, 1987. By permission.

A MEDIEVAL FAIR

HOW TO GO ABOUT IT

Beforehand

■ Set a date, arrange for the "fairgrounds," and schedule custodial help. (Our custodians have been invaluable in "planting" posts and in cleaning and trimming grounds.)

■ Schedule times for guests to come to the fair. (We have guests attend in two shifts to make the fair more manageable.)

■ Be sure that "money" has been printed and delivered.

■ Be sure that any prizes to be awarded to visitors have been prepared.

■ Organize and "coach" a set-up and take-down crew of students.

OUR FAIR LAYOUT

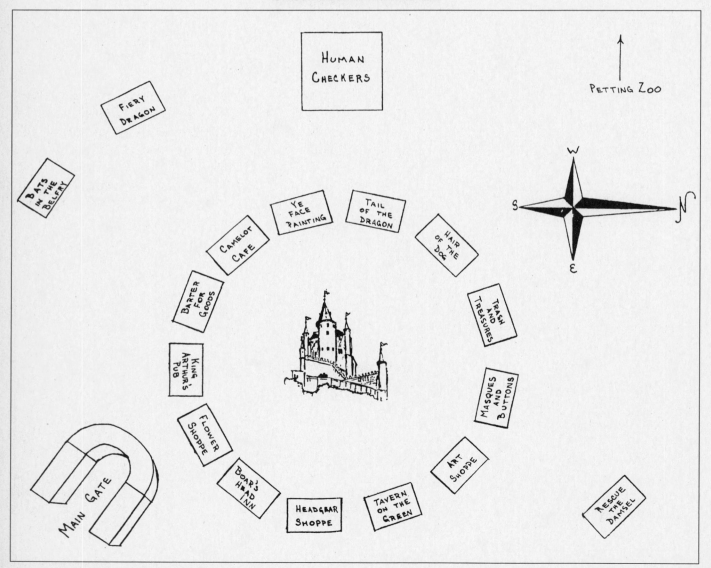

1. Fair Booths

For our fair, we set up the following booths.

Three drink booths:

- King Arthur's Pub
- Hair of the Dog
- Tavern on the Green

Three food booths:

- Camelot Cafe
- Tail of the Dragon
- Boar's Head Inn

Several crafts booths:

- Headgear Shoppe (We sell Robin Hood and Damsel hats.)
- Ye Masques and Buttons (Our "masques" are made from wallpaper glued to cardboard, into which feathers are inserted. Buttons are made from Medieval pictures that students have colored.)
- The Art Shoppe (Students' artwork is displayed in the gallery. Tables are set up for visitors to make brass rubbings and stained glass window-drawings.)
- Ye Jewelry (Students create wire jewelry while guests wait.)
- The Flower Shoppe (We sell tissue-paper flowers.)
- Barter for Goods (We sell "white elephants" donated by students and teachers.)
- Trash 'n' Treasures (More "white elephants" are sold here.)

Specialty booths:

- Ye Make-Up (Students paint the faces of guests.)
- The Fortune Teller (Our seer used a "Magic 8 Ball" to answer guests' questions.)
- Ye Medieval Weaponry (Parent-volunteers make swords and axes out of heavy cardboard, which they paint. Maces can be made from dowels, string, Styrofoam balls, and toothpicks. This shop sells out quickly!)

2. Games and Activities

All games used at our fair are created by students. We usually include the following activities.

- Human Checkers (This requires twenty-four checkers and two callers. We make simple vests in two colors to distinguish each side. We use cardboard crowns for "kings." You may want to have students practice this activity beforehand. Select "teams" from among those students who seem to enjoy the activity.)
- Jousts (Riders and cardboard horses compete in a mock joust.)
- Medieval Theater (Students read excerpts from and/or put on dramatic presentations of stories set in the Middle Ages.)
- Medieval Minstrels (Our music teacher helps student-minstrels provide musical interludes.)
- Petting Zoo (One of our counselors raises miniature horses and pot-bellied pigs! This is a favorite with younger guests.)

3. Fair Time

On a given signal, the set-up crew puts the booths, tables, murals, and banners in place. Then a signal is given for the first shift, whereupon "sentinels," "vendors," and "serfs" take goods to the appropriate booths, get the ice, and stock their booths.

As the first guests arrive through the castle gates, students and teachers, hopefully all in costume, start greeting and hawking in "Old English" style. Adults circulate around the fairgrounds, checking on booths and providing help where needed.

Our "Human Checker" teams, who have previously been coached, now perform at the scheduled time—much to the pleasure of the visitors. The arrival of the King (our school principal) is a much awaited event. The King is honored by our students by being offered food, a beverage, and an opportunity to participate in one of the gaming events.

Our games are especially popular with the visitors. Prizes, which have been prepared by students beforehand, are awarded for winning or participation. Our Medieval money is worth three marks (punches). Usually a drink is worth one punch, and a food or craft might be worth two or three punches. (Each student starts out with one piece of Medieval money, but there are opportunities to earn others.)

4. In Conclusion

The last guests are ushered out. You may want to allow 15 to 20 minutes for your own students to enjoy what is left and start the clean-up.

Take the leftover goods and booths back to the classrooms for storage or later disposal. If soda and non-perishables are left, they can be used at a later party.

In your next class time with students, you may debrief and evaluate. Students take the evaluation process very seriously, and their responses are candid and insightful. We have incorporated many of their ideas into our fairs.

Our team has been holding Medieval Fairs for seven years now. The fair has grown, just as we have. The suggestions we make here have become a tradition for us. We hope you'll pick and choose those ideas that appeal to you— and add other ideas of your own. Our best advice is to relax and enjoy and trust your kids. They'll make sure their fair works!

Dale

MEDIEVAL TIMES: A MINI-MUSEUM

Throughout this unit, students have participated in many hands-on activities to create a Medieval environment. This culmination gives students an opportunity to show off their work to best advantage. Students choose the items they wish to display in their mini-museum; they also make live presentations that may include dramatic re-enactments based on the literature they've read.

When You Can Use It
★ Culmination

What Leads Up To It
■ Student Project
■ All Instructional Activities that involve hands-on projects as well as the literature-based lessons

What You'll Need
■ Samples of students' work
■ Tables for display
■ An area to act as a stage for dramatic presentations

HOW TO GO ABOUT IT

1. Ask students to share any experiences they may have had visiting art museums or museums of natural history. Encourage them to describe displays that were of particular interest to them. Then tell students that they will create their own museum exhibits, filled with the Medieval things they have produced during this unit. Point out that in addition to the models they have made, students will display their own thespian talents.

2. Suggest that students spend some time thinking about what they want to display in their exhibits. Encourage them to choose from among their best work. They might make maps or charts to present interesting information they learned during the unit; these might focus on castle construction, the Crusades, the Black Death, and so on. Students should also create a name for their museum, as well as titles for the various exhibits.

3. Allow plenty of time for students to set up their exhibits and to rehearse their performances. You might have a "public relations" team arrange for publicity and sending out invitations. (If students have developed skill with calligraphy, this would be a good time to apply it!)

4. Discuss with students possible roles they might play once their guests arrive. Some might serve as docents, giving informal talks about the various displays. Others might act as hosts, especially if any refreshments are to be served.

5. Consider having a "dress rehearsal" for the grand opening of the museum. This will enable students on the team to be the first to tour through it.

MEDIEVAL TALES: PUTTING ON A PAGEANT

In their Medieval roles, students have created stories that they have presented in writing, graphically, or through dramatic presentations. Students can use their stories to put on a Medieval pageant— with or without costumes. This is a relatively simple culminating experience that enables students to present work they've already done to a larger audience.

When You Can Use It
★ Culmination

What Leads Up To It
■ Student Project
■ All Instructional Activities

What You 'll Need
■ A stage or large area for individual and/or group presentations
■ Optional: costumes
■ Optional: prepared awards or certificates for students

HOW TO GO ABOUT IT

1. This Culminating Experience enables students to share the Medieval stories they have developed in this unit with other classes or with a parent audience. It can be done as simply or elaborately as you and your students want.

2. The structure of the presentation will depend on what media students have used to tell their stories. If most or all of the students have used some form of graphic presentation (a storyboard, mural, or diorama), the previous Culminating Experience (Medieval Times: A Mini-Museum) may be more appropriate. Regardless of what kind of presentation you have planned, remember to include some live or recorded music. Music is great for evoking another time and any of the recordings listed in "Listening to Medieval Music" on page 76 will work very effectively.

3. If most or all of the students have told their stories on paper (as a short story, a journalistic account, a play, or a poem or song), you might have students pick the best story and present a dramatization of it, using the guidelines provided for "The Play's the Thing!" on page 84. Another possibility is to have a series of readings of poems and stories with musical interludes.

4. The various dramatic presentations shown on page 20 in the Student Project Book (a play, a puppet show, a radio program, a video) are obviously ideal for this Culminating Experience. To maximize the size and enthusiasm of your audience, you might send out invitations and prepare posters to advertise the event. Including an RSVP on the invitations helps to ensure a good turnout.

5. There's no need to make the pageant too solemn. The miracle plays that were performed on the steps of Medieval cathedrals mixed drama and comedy freely. It was not unusual for an actor playing the role of a demon to descend from the stage and prod members of the audience with a pitchfork. We don't recommend this, but you might tell students that Medieval drama had many humorous elements, including slapstick and juggling.

6. One way to make any presentation more memorable is to provide refreshments. Students might enjoy preparing some of the fare described in Madeleine Cosman's *Fabulous Feasts* (see Bibliography for details).

A MEDIEVAL TAPESTRY

This culminating experience provides students an opportunity to create a visual interpretation of the Middle Ages. In their Medieval roles, students design and execute panels of a tapestry, which can be displayed in any large area (such as a hallway or cafeteria).

When You Can Use It
★ Culmination

What Leads Up To It
■ Student Project
■ All Instructional Activities

What You'll Need
■ Art supplies
■ Large sheets of butcher paper

HOW TO GO ABOUT IT

1. Share several pictures of Medieval tapestries with students. Discuss the decorative motifs used, pointing out any scenes of everyday life that may be represented. (Most Medieval tapestries showed scenes from history, from mythology, or from everyday life.) Explain to students that tapestry-making is a very old art, and that most tapestry weavers work from a full-size "cartoon," or drawing, done by another artist.

2. Point out that although a tapestry is a woven fabric, usually used as a wallhanging, students can create a similar effect using large sheets of butcher paper and paints (or other media). Gather art supplies and, if possible, enlist the aid of exploratory teachers. Have students decide how they wish to work to create their own tapestries. Students who have assumed similar Medieval roles may want to work together.

3. Suggest that students prepare several sketches of what they might show on their tapestries. Have them review the pages of their Student Project Book to decide what aspect of their Medieval lives they want to highlight. Set up some guidelines for overall size of the finished products.

4. Once students have decided on the content of their tapestries, they can begin to transfer their ideas onto large sheets of butcher paper. Allow students to decide for themselves the media to be used: paints, pastels, colored markers, or crayons.

UTOPIA: IMAGINING A BETTER WORLD

In this culminating experience, students brainstorm with classmates to create their own perfect social and political system. This is one of the most stimulating activities for both students and teachers. The thoughtfulness and sheer ingenuity of the "ideal civilizations" should impress you—and, quite often, make you laugh!

When You Can Use It
★ Culmination

What Leads Up To It
■ Student Projects
■ All Instructional Activities

HOW TO GO ABOUT IT

1. Have students brainstorm about the positive and negative changes that have occurred in the world in their lifetime. Ask them to think about how their civilization could be improved. Then discuss the meaning of the word *utopia*, perhaps quoting its definition from the dictionary. Ask volunteers to define *utopia* in their own words.

2. Familiarize students with the name Sir Thomas More. Point out that in 1516, More wrote a satire in which he conceived his own "perfect" political, economic, and social system. He called the book *Utopia*, after the name of the imaginary island on which he established his own ideal world.

3. Have students imagine an ideal civilization or utopia of their own. To get them started, suggest that they use a web with the following elements: name of civilization, education,

laws, location, people, government, currency, occupations, and recreation. Circulate among the groups as students work; provide assistance, as needed.

4. Ask students to describe their civilizations in short essays, and then have them share their work with classmates. Remind them that there is no "wrong" or "right" when it comes to imagining a utopia.

5. Students might also like to research Edward Bellamy (1850-1898), who described an American Utopia. In his novel *Looking Backward*, he tells the story of a Boston man who falls asleep in 1887 and awakens in the years 2000. The United States has created a perfect socialist state where poverty, ignorance, and crime have all be eliminated.

EVALUATING
YOUR UNIT

Take time to reflect...

EVALUATE STUDENT PERFORMANCE

What items and aspects of your students' work you decide to evaluate depends greatly on your unit objectives and on whether your unit supplements your regular curriculum or supplants it. How you perform the evaluation also depends on two key factors: (1) whether you want to grade individually by subject or by group consensus on overall unit goals and (2) the evaluation system in place in your school or district. The only aspect of evaluation that's not a mystery is *when*—you determine what to evaluate at the beginning of the your unit to prevent headaches at the end!

EVALUATION TOOLS IN THIS UNIT

Built into this Resource Unit are tools to help you organize your evaluation program. Which ones you decide to use and how you choose to use them depend on:

- **your team goals.** Is this unit reinforcing previously taught content and skills? Or is it introducing them? Will this unit "count" toward students' grades in each subject area? How?

- **the role of assessment in your school and/or district.** Do you need to measure the retention and comprehension of specific content in this unit?

Once you've determined the importance of this unit in your overall curriculum and have specified what your team's academic and affective goals are, you'll have concrete yardsticks for determining what, how much, and how often you'll evaluate during the course of the unit. Because assessment needs and systems vary so widely among middle schools and even among teachers on the same team, the tools we've provided for your use can be adapted to suit your particular situation.

Objectives Checklist, page 110. This blackline master is designed to highlight the correspondence between your academic and affective goals for the unit and the activities you selected. By completing this checklist, you'll have an at-a-glance reference of which activities are most important to assess and, if you're using a portfolio system, to include in students' portfolios.

Student Contract, page 112. This contract is designed to help you and your students talk explicitly about unit requirements.

Once you've determined the scope and sequence of your unit with your team, you'll be able to assign points to each required item or activity. Think about whether you'll award points based simply on task completion or on pre-determined levels of quality. To prevent frustration, explain both the points and the quality levels to students before they commit to their responsibilities.

In place of the contract (or in conjunction with it), you might use the Unit Schedule (page 106) as a way of soliciting and documenting student responsibilities. Including both of these items in students' on-going portfolios allows you to chart students' growth in their ability to follow through with responsibilities.

Student Self-Evaluation. This worksheet in the Student Project Book (pages 22) is a way for students to reflect on their own learning. The effectiveness of this tool can be enhanced if students are encouraged to set personal learning goals at the beginning of the unit. That way, they can measure their learning as they go along. Students' thoughts about their own work are particularly valuable additions to their portfolios.

This worksheet can be used to measure not only the success of students' achievements, but also your success as well! We've found that student comments (that is, their criticisms and suggestions) help us refine our unit from year to year.

Activity Bank, pages 47-94. Most activities contain tips on what you might assess. These tips are tied directly to the stated skill or strategy objectives for the activity. Of course, because the activities can be customized in a variety of ways—both in terms of unit content and in skills that can be emphasized in the different subject areas—what you assess will depend greatly on how you go about the activity! The tips are a starting point for you.

The instructional activities are opportunities not only for traditional evaluation of content acquisition and understanding, but also for on-going, authentic assessment of students' written, oral, and visual presentation skills and strategies

Teacher Team Notes. This Student Project Book page (page 23) is the place for each team member to respond to students' work during the student project and/or in individual subject-area classes. Because this page is part of each student's book, it is a marvelous opportunity to give positive feedback and suggestions for future reference. The entire project book, complete with student and teacher evaluation, can also be shared with families as a way of documenting student growth.

Student Evaluation Form, page 111. This blackline master is the place to summarize the information gleaned from all sources. The form has space for you to summarize your assessment of the student's:

- fulfillment of his/her contract
- work to be included in his/her portfolio
- view of his/her work

You might include this form in the student's cumulative files, share it with parents at a future parent-teacher conference and/or with the student during an individual conference.

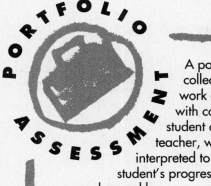

A portfolio is a collection of a student's work over time, along with comments from the student and from the teacher, which can be interpreted to give a view of the student's progress. Portfolios can be used by:

- **students and teachers**—to assess student progress, to individualize instruction, and to set and monitor learning goals

- **parents**—to appreciate their child's learning and development

- **administrators**—to assess the scope of your curriculum

- **students' future teachers**—to ensure continuity and to understand students' needs and talents

The best way to collect items for the portfolios is to allow students to participate in the selection process. Ask them to select items that they feel represent their best work and to write why they think it's good or what it shows about their growth.

Useful items to include:

- photocopies of Student Project Book pages 6-21, as a record of their thinking and their research during the project. (Photocopies allow the student to keep the book intact and ready to refer to in the future.)

- the Student Self-Evaluation

- the Student Contract

- photographs of student work during the culminating experience—products and performance. Photographs are especially helpful in highlighting affective details—enthusiasm, participation, etc.

TEAM MEETING

HOW DID OUR KIDS DO?

Take some time to recall the highlights of your unit. Then use the reproducible form on the next page to make team decisions about individual student progress toward your unit objectives. You may want to collect the Student Project Books before this team meeting. Divide the books among team members for review.

1 UNIT OBJECTIVES
Review your Objectives Checklist and consider students' progress toward your goals.

2 SUBJECT-AREA CLASSES
It's hard to assign separate subject-area grades for content in a truly interdisciplinary unit. You might assign such grades for discipline-specific skills covered in class activities. Then you can feel free to award a team grade on the concepts and content presented in all the instructional activities.

3 STUDENT SUCCESS
Refer to the Evaluation pages in the Student Project Books (pages 22-23). You might also make notes for next year on individual Activity Bank pages, as well as on your Unit Curriculum Planner.

4 CONTRACTS/SCHEDULES
As you discuss students' schedules, consider their work loads and the time allotted to homework and to the student project.

5 FEEDBACK
Will you emphasize:
Participation?
Performance?
End project(s)?
Process?

1 **How well did we achieve our unit objectives?**

INSTRUCTIONAL
ACTIVITIES:

CULMINATING
EXPERIENCES:

STUDENT
PROJECTS:

2 **How well did students do in our subject-area classes?**
Will we give separate grades and/or an overall unit grade?

SCIENCE:

SOCIAL STUDIES:

MATH:

ENGLISH/LITERATURE:

3 **In which activities did students do especially well? Why?**

4 **How well did students fulfill their contracts and/or**
meet their schedules? What can we do next time to help
them be even more successful?

5 **What kind of feedback will we give students in our**
Teacher Team Notes?

TEAM MEETING

HOW DID WE DO?

Think about all the behind-the-scenes work your team has done to get ready for this unit and to carry it off. Take some time now to reflect on your own experiences, noting what worked and what didn't. You may find the reproducible form on the next page useful in recording your thoughts.

1 PREPARATION
Did the ideas you came up with in brainstorming help you shape the unit effectively? Why or why not? Did the customizing process help you determine priorities? Review your Objectives Checklist and consider students' progress toward your goals.

2 TIME ALLOTMENT
Did you accomplish everything you set out to? How did the unit stack up against your master schedule? When did you run short of time?

3 MANAGEMENT
Did all participants (including students) understand their roles in the unit? Where were the "rough spots"? How could they be smoothed out next time?

4 TEAM MEETING
Did you assign each team member a role for the team meetings? How did that work? Was it possible to have regularly scheduled meetings?

5 EVALUATION
Was the evaluation process manageable for the team as a whole? Did establishing guidelines up front work well for you?

1 How well did our planning time prepare us for the unit?

2 How well did we estimate and allot our time?

TO PREPARE FOR THE UNIT:

TO MANAGE THE UNIT:

TO ASSESS THE UNIT AS IT PROGRESSED:

3 How well did we manage the unit? Did things always run smoothly?

4 Were our team meetings frequent enough? Did we always state and accomplish our goals for these meetings?

5 How well did our evaluation system work?

TEAM MEETING

WHAT WILL WE DO DIFFERENTLY NEXT TIME?

On the basis of your own and your students' assessment of the unit, what lessons did you learn that can help you carry out this unit again? Use this reproducible form to capture your thoughts while they're still fresh to save you time and energy the next time around! (This form also appears in Team Tools, page 116.)

1 *Launch Activity:*

2 *Instructional Activities:*

3 *Student Project:*

4 *Culminating Experience:*

5 *Team Planning Process:*

TEAM
T O O L S

Forms, Charts, Schedules

Reproducible forms to help you develop and carry out your unit year after year!

UNIT CURRICULUM PLANNER

Who were the people of the Middle Ages?

INSTRUCTIONAL ACTIVITIES:

LAUNCH

STUDENT PROJECT:

How was Medieval society organized?

INSTRUCTIONAL ACTIVITIES:

STUDENT PROJECT:

What was life like then?

INSTRUCTIONAL ACTIVITIES:

STUDENT PROJECT:

What values and ideas were important in Medieval culture?

INSTRUCTIONAL ACTIVITIES:

STUDENT PROJECT:

How did people in the Middle Ages help shape our world today?

INSTRUCTIONAL ACTIVITIES:

STUDENT PROJECT:

CULMINATING EXPERIENCE

UNIT SCHEDULE

MONTH _____ YEAR _____

MONDAY

TUESDAY

WEDNESDAY

THURSDAY

FRIDAY

SATURDAY

SUNDAY

ACTIVITY PLAN A

	MONDAY	TUESDAY	WEDNESDAY	THURSDAY	FRIDAY
SCIENCE					
MATH					
SOCIAL STUDIES					
ENGLISH					
LITERATURE					

ACTIVITY PLAN B

Date of Activity	Activity/What Will Be Assessed	Teacher Responsible for Activity	Materials and Equipment Needed	Resource People Needed	Other

ACTIVITY PLAN C

	STUDENT PROJECT		INSTRUCTIONAL ACTIVITIES		
	Activity	Check Point(s)	Activity	Subject Area	Evaluation
Monday					
Tuesday					
Wednesday					
Thursday					
Friday					

OBJECTIVES CHECKLIST

Along the top of the chart, fill in the skill, content, and affective objectives you want to emphasize in this unit. Then fill in the activities you've selected, checking to see that each objective is met by at least one activity.

STUDENT EVALUATION FORM

Use this form to pull together your thoughts about the activities and items you've evaluated for your students. You can use this information:

- to determine a final grade for the unit
- as part of students' on-going portfolios
- to keep parents informed

STUDENT: _____

Student Contract   Points/Grade

   Non-Negotiable Items:

   Negotiable Items:

   Demonstration of Learning:

Portfolio Items   Grade

   Item: _____

   Item: _____

   Item: _____

   Item: _____

   Item: _____

Student's Self-Evaluation

   Key Ideas:

STUDENT CONTRACT
OF ACCEPTANCE

On this day, _____, 19 ____, I, _____, being of sound mind and body, do hereby agree to complete the following tasks to the best of my ability.

Non-Negotiable

A. Work through the five questions of the Student Project Book and complete My Medieval Story (pages 19-21).
B. Participate in the culminating experience.
C. Complete the unit evaluation (page 22).

Negotiable

A. Build a scale model of a Medieval town and/or castle.
B. Read two books (fiction or nonfiction) about the Middle Ages.
C. Use a card catalog, the *Readers' Guide to Periodical Literature*, or a computer data base to locate information.
D. _____
E. _____
F. _____

Demonstration of Learning

To demonstrate what I have learned, I will do the following:

_____
_____
_____

I will stay on task in class, working alone or with others. I understand that work not completed during class time must be done at home. Contract rules have been explained, and I understand them.

X _____ (student)

I will give necessary help and support. I will review and return any work quickly and effectively.

X _____ (team representative)

Certificate of Achievement

This certifies that

_____

(name)

has explored the Middle Ages and has

demonstrated an understanding of the impact

_____ of that era on our modern world.

The Middle Ages

Signed _____

on the _____ day of

_____, _____.

TEACHER RESOURCE NOTES

How many times have you found the perfect resource only to find later on that you can't remember where it was located? Use this page to jot down those "too-good-to-be-true" resources that you will want to call on again. It might be a person, a place, or a book. But now it will be right here at your fingertips!

RESOURCE	LOCATION	TO USE FOR

TEAM MEETING

TEAM MEETING

Date

Time

Place

OUR GOAL FOR THE MEETING

TASKS TO DO BEFORE THE MEETING

1

2

3

4

5

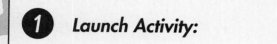

TEAM MEETING

1 *Launch Activity:*

2 *Instructional Activities:*

3 *Student Project:*

4 *Culminating Experience:*

5 *Team Planning Process:*

K-W-L STRATEGY SHEET

K WHAT WE KNOW

W WHAT WE WANT TO FIND OUT

L WHAT WE LEARNED

CATEGORIES OF INFORMATION

A.
B.
C.
D.

CATEGORIES OF INFORMATION

E.
F.

Teacher's Group Observation Sheet

Groups	Explains Concepts	Encourages Participation	Checks Understanding	Organizes the Work
1				
2				
3				
4				
5				

Bibliography—Resources for Teachers

(For books for students, please see pages 46-47 of the Student Project Book.)

—Books—

Armstrong, Karen. *Holy War: The Crusades and Their Impact on Today's World.* Doubleday, 1991. A fascinating look at how the Crusades created much of the distrust between the Christian and Arab worlds today. "Any reader will come away from this book," wrote the *Kansas City Star*, "with a better frame of reference for assessing today's headlines." A useful resource for connecting past and present.

Bayard, Tania (translator and editor). *A Medieval Home Companion: Housekeeping in the Fourteenth Century.* Harper Perennial, 1992. In the 1390s a 15-year-old girl in Paris married an older man. As a wedding present, he wrote her a book telling everything he knew about running a household, from how to graft a cherry tree to the care of fine furs.

Bishop, Morris. *The Middle Ages.* Houghton, Mifflin, 1987. One of the best introductions to the Middle Ages currently available. From details of everyday life to the complexities of Medieval politics, Morris provides a comprehensive view of the Middle Ages with plenty of wit.

Black, Maggie. *The Medieval Cookbook.* Thames and Hudson, 1992. Eighty recipes from Medieval manuscripts, adapted for the modern kitchen, including foods eaten by all levels of society.

Bogin, Meg. *The Women Troubadours.* Norton, 1980. Recent scholarship has revealed that a number of troubadours in 12th- and 13th-century France were women. Bogin explains the importance of these poets and provides a generous selection of their writings. American poet Adrienne Rich says, "Bogin has unearthed one of the strongest and loveliest of the varied fragments of women's culture."

Boyer, Carl B. *A History of Mathematics.* John Wiley and Sons, 1991. A good general history that describes the important advances made by Medieval mathematicians.

Cantor, Normal F. *The Civilization of the Middle Ages.* Harper Perennial, 1993. An excellent overview of Medieval society. *Booklist* wrote, "No better explanation of medievalism is available for the general reader."

Cantor, Norman F. *Medieval Lives: Eight Charismatic Men and Women of the Middle Ages.* Harper Collins, 1994. Highly readable sketches of eight prominent Medieval men and women, including Eleanor of Aquitaine, Augustine of Hippo, and Robert Grosseteste (the founder of experimental science).

Cohen, Barbara. *Canterbury Tales.* Illustrated by Trina Schart Hyman. Morrow, 1988. A well-done retelling of four of Chaucer's tales.

Cosman, Madeleine Pelner. *Fabulous Feasts: Medieval Cookery and Ceremony.* Braziller, 1976. A guide to preparing everything from a Medieval punch to a full dinner.

Drogin, Marc. *Medieval Calligraphy: Its History and Technique.* Dover, 1989. A combination history and instruction manual that shows how to reproduce 13 medieval scripts.

Gies, Frances and Joseph. *Cathedral, Forge, and Waterwheel: Technology and Invention in the Middle Ages.* Harper Collins, 1994. In this, the eighth book they have written together about the Middle Ages, the Gies use recent scholarship to show how Medieval inventions laid the foundation for the Industrial Revolution. They also demonstrate that many of these innovations—the horse harness, the compass, and the use of cotton, for example—originated in the East. Illustrated.

Gies, Frances and Joseph. *Life in a Medieval City.* Harper Perennial, 1991. A study of life in Troyes, capital of the county of Champagne in France, the site of the largest Medieval fairs. Includes useful information about both the "Hot Fair" in August and the "Cold Fair" in December.

Gimpel, Jean. *The Medieval Machine: The Industrial Revolution of the Middle Ages.* Penguin Books, 1977. Explains how Medieval farming, construction, and industry were transformed by new forms of energy and machinery.

Giulio, Cattin. *Music of the Middle Ages* (translated by Steven Botterill). Cambridge University Press, 1984. Tells how Gregorian chant developed from a mixture of Eastern and Western traditions.

Gottfried, Robert S. *The Black Death.* Free Press, 1983. How did a disease that had existed for thousands of years suddenly spread across Europe and Asia, killing millions of people? A medical detective book that provides some persuasive answers to that question.

Hanawalt, Barbara A. *Growing Up in Medieval London.* Oxford University Press, 1994. Composite profiles of young people living in 14th- and 15th-century London drawn from the experiences of real children.

Holmes, George (editor). *The Oxford History of Medieval Europe.* Oxford University Press, 1992. A good, introduction to Medieval history.

Holt, J.C. *Robin Hood.* Thames and Hudson, 1989. Who was the real Robin Hood? The answer is supplied by this Medieval scholar at Cambridge University who served as the historical advisor for the 1991 film *Robin Hood* (see below). The British newspaper *The Observer* called his book "the last word on Robin Hood."

Komroff, Manuel (translator and editor). *The Travels of Marco Polo.* Liveright, 1982. This book lets your students hear about Polo's exploits in his own words.

Labarge, Margaret Wade. *A Small Sound of the Trumpet: Women in Medieval Life.* Beacon Press, 1986. A trailblazing study of the role of Medieval women.

McEvedy, Colin. *The New Penguin Atlas of Medieval History.* Penguin Books, 1992. A collection of 45 two-color maps that show the progress of Medieval history and provide information about the geography of Europe.

Rowling, Marjorie. *Life in Medieval Times.* Putnam, 1979. This look at life during the Middle Ages is enhanced by abundant quotations from Medieval poets, historians, and other writers.

Sancha, Sheila. *The Luttrell Village: Country Life in the Middle Ages.* Harper Collins, 1982. The popular illustrated book about life in an English village in the 14th century. Also available in a Spanish-language edition from Lectorum Books, New York.

Sancha, Sheila. *Walter Dragun's Town.* Harper Collins, 1989. The whole world of a Medieval town, from young apprentices to master craftspeople.

Snyder, James. *Medieval Art: Painting, Sculpture, Architecture.* Harry N. Abrams, 1989. An excellent, illustrated overview of Medieval art.

Stanton, Domna C. *The Defiant Muse: French Feminist Poems from the Middle Ages to the Present.* The Feminist Press of the City University of New York, 1986. Includes translations of the work of de Pisan and other women poets of the Middle Ages.

Toy, Sidney. *Castles: Their Construction and History.* Dover Publications, 1984. A classic study of how castles were built and how castle construction developed from structures used by the Greeks and Romans.

Wilson, Christopher. *The Gothic Cathedral.* Thames and Hudson, 1990. A superb book, illustrated with line drawings and black-and-white photographs, that draws on the latest work of art researchers.

The Ballad of Robin Hood. performed by Anthony Quayle. Caedmon SWC 1177 (47 min.) The famous British actor reads the popular ballads that created the Robin Hood legend.

Chaucer, Geoffrey. **The Canterbury Tales in Middle English** performed by J.B. Bessinger, Jr. Caedmon SWC 1151 (45 min.) Chaucer's classic in its original Middle English. You'll be surprised how much you can understand if you follow along with a modern translation.

—Videocassettes—

Brother Sun, Sister Moon. Directed by Franco Zefferelli. This 1969 film, Zefferelli's first after his classic version of *Romeo and Juliet*, tells the story of St. Francis of Assisi (121 min.). Rated PG.

Castle. Illustrator David Macaulay shows students how castles were built in fascinating detail. Based on his popular book of the same name. Both are available from the Social Studies School Service of Culver City CA (57 min.).

Cathedral: The Story of Its Construction. David Macaulay leads students through some of the most magnificent cathedrals of France, explaining the engineering skill behind their beauty. Distributed by Social Studies School Service (58 min.).

The First Secular Music (Part of the acclaimed *Music in Time* series). Renowned flutist James Galway will take your students on a tour of early music, tracing its roots and showing how it flowered throughout Medieval Europe. The program includes traditional Gregorian, Hebrew, and Greek chants (60 min.). Distributed by Films for the Humanities and Sciences of Princeton, NJ.

The Torment of Joan of Arc: You Are There. Host Walter Chronkite shows how TV might have covered the trial of Joan of Arc. Produced By CBS News (22 min.). Distributed by Social Studies School Service.

The Lion in Winter. Directed by James Goldman. Katherine Hepburn stars as the legendary Eleanor of Aquitaine and Peter O'Toole plays King Henry in this superb 1970 film (134 min.).

Medieval Times: 1000-1450. This concise single-cassette program from United Learning uses live-action dramatizations to show what Medieval daily life was like in castles, manor farms, villages, and monasteries (31 min.) Distributed by Social Studies School Service.

The Middle Ages. This is an excellent series of five 20-minute video programs from the BBC that combines effective dramatic scenes with documentary footage of castles, cathedrals, and battle-grounds. The segments explore the following topics: "The Peasants' Revolt," "The Castle," "The Church," "The Town," and "The Traders" (100 min. total). Distributed by Social Studies School Service.

Robin Hood. Patrick Bergin stars in an atmospheric retelling of the Robin Hood story from 1991. Lots of action, great photography, and surprisingly accurate in its portrayal of the conflicts between Normans and Britons (150 min.).

—Other Resources—

Magna Carta Kit. Includes a fascimile of the famous document, a translation, six other primary source exhibits, six broadsheets, a reading list, and teaching notes. Created by Golden Owl and distributed by Social Studies School Service.

Medieval Charts. A series of four charts with teaching notes on "Medieval Castles, "Medieval Monasticism," "Medieval Village Life," and "A Medieval Town." Charts created by Pictorial Charts in London and distributed by Social Studies School Service.

The Medieval Woman: An Illuminated Calendar. A beautiful four-color calendar featuring images from Medieval manuscripts. Available from Workman Publishing, 708 Broadway, New York NY 10003 (212) 614-7580.